KID CONFIDENT #1

How to Manage Your
Social Power
in Middle School

KID CONFIDENT #1

How to Manage Your
Social Power
in Middle School

by Bonnie Zucker, PsyD   illustrated by DeAndra Hodge

Magination Press · Washington, DC · American Psychological Association

is a gift that I treasure every day. Thank you for teaching me the value and
meaning of true friendship, and for always loving me as I am. I love you
more than words can say—*BZ*

To my mom and big brother for their love and support—*DH*

Magination Press
Books for Kids From the American Psychological Association

Copyright © 2022 by Bonnie Zucker. Illustrations copyright © 2022 by DeAndra Hodge. Published in 2022 by Magination Press, an imprint of the American Psychological Association. All rights reserved. Except as permitted under the United States Copyright Act of 1976, no part of this publication may be reproduced or distributed in any form or by any means, or stored in a database or retrieval system, without the prior written permission of the publisher.

Magination Press is a registered trademark of the American Psychological Association. Order books at maginationpress.org or call 1-800-374-2721.

Series editor: Bonnie Zucker, PsyD
Book design: Rachel Ross
Printed by Lake Book Manufacturing, Inc., Melrose Park, IL
Library of Congress Cataloging-in-Publication Data
Names: Zucker, Bonnie, 1974- author. | Hodge, DeAndra, illustrator.
Title: Kid confident #1: how to manage your social power in middle school / by Bonnie Zucker, PsyD; illustrations by DeAndra Hodge.
Description: Washington, DC: Magination Press, [2022] | Summary: "Kid Confident explains the dynamic of social power, equal and unequal, in the context of friendships and with unfriendly peers"—Provided by publisher.
Identifiers: LCCN 2022001661 (print) | LCCN 2022001662 (ebook) | ISBN 9781433838149 (hardback) | ISBN 9781433838156 (ebook)
Subjects: LCSH: Self-confidence—Juvenile literature. | Power (Social sciences)—Juvenile literature. | Friendship—Sociological aspect—Juvenile literature.
Classification: LCC BF575.S39 Z83 2022 (print) | LCC BF575.S39 (ebook) | DDC 155.4/182—dc23/eng/20220114
LC record available at https://lccn.loc.gov/2022001661
LC ebook record available at https://lccn.loc.gov/2022001662
Manufactured in the United States of America
10 9 8 7 6 5 4 3 2 1

CONTENTS

Dear Reader (Don't Skip This!) — 7

A Note for the Adults in Your Life — 11

Chapter 1.
Social Power Defined — 15

Chapter 2.
Know Your Rights & Be Assertive — 43

Chapter 3.
Discover Self-Confidence & Self-Control — 75

Chapter 4.
Find Mutual Respect & Generosity — 103

Chapter 5.
Rebalance Power Imbalances & Struggles — 121

Chapter 6.
Inspiring Stories — 131

Chapter 7.
Practice Takes Practice — 153

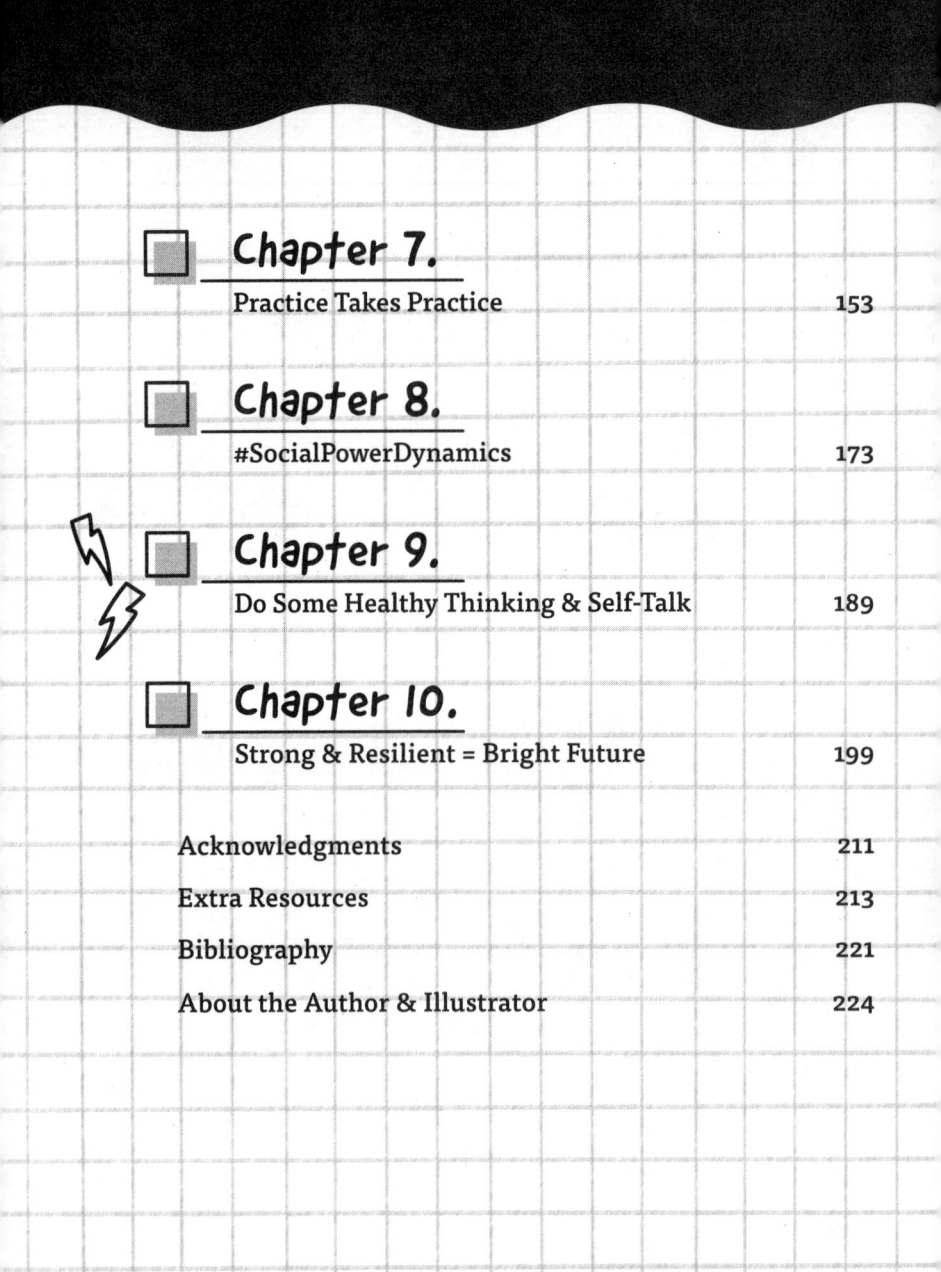

Chapter 8.
#SocialPowerDynamics — 173

Chapter 9.
Do Some Healthy Thinking & Self-Talk — 189

Chapter 10.
Strong & Resilient = Bright Future — 199

Acknowledgments — 211
Extra Resources — 213
Bibliography — 221
About the Author & Illustrator — 224

Dear Reader (Don't Skip This!)

You've probably never heard of the term **social power** before, but I'm sure you've experienced it many times in your life. Whether it is equal or unequal, social power plays a role in both friendships and non-friend peer relationships you have. When the power between you is balanced and equal, you feel awesome:

- you will thrive in your friendships and relationships,
- you will know yourself the most,
- you become the best version of yourself,
- and you have a solid sense of confidence.

When it's out of balance and someone has or tries to have power over you, it creates an **UNBALANCED, UNEQUAL DYNAMIC** which causes you to feel stress, sadness, embarrassment, and even feelings of vulnerability and powerlessness.

Doesn't sound too fun, does it?

Well, this book is here to help. I will guide you through the process of understanding what social power is, how it comes up in relationships, and how to navigate your way through social power struggles or when things get unbalanced.

As you learn the best approach to managing social power issues, you will develop several key skills that will not only help you with this dynamic, but will benefit you in the long-run as you become an older teen and, eventually, an adult. These skills include

- learning how to be **ASSERTIVE,**
- demonstrating **SELF-CONFIDENCE,**
- focusing on how to **CHANGE YOUR EXPERIENCE** in any situation, and
- responding according to your **PERSONAL VALUE SYSTEM,** rather than your feelings.

I know that guide books, or self-help books such as this one, might not be the thing you run home and rush to do, but I promise you that you won't regret reading it and learning the most effective approach to handling social power in your life. To make it as engaging as possible, I was sure to include plenty of illustrations, graphics, and other fun features. So, let's get started so you can be on your way to mastering the world of social power. Good luck!

—**Bonnie Z.**

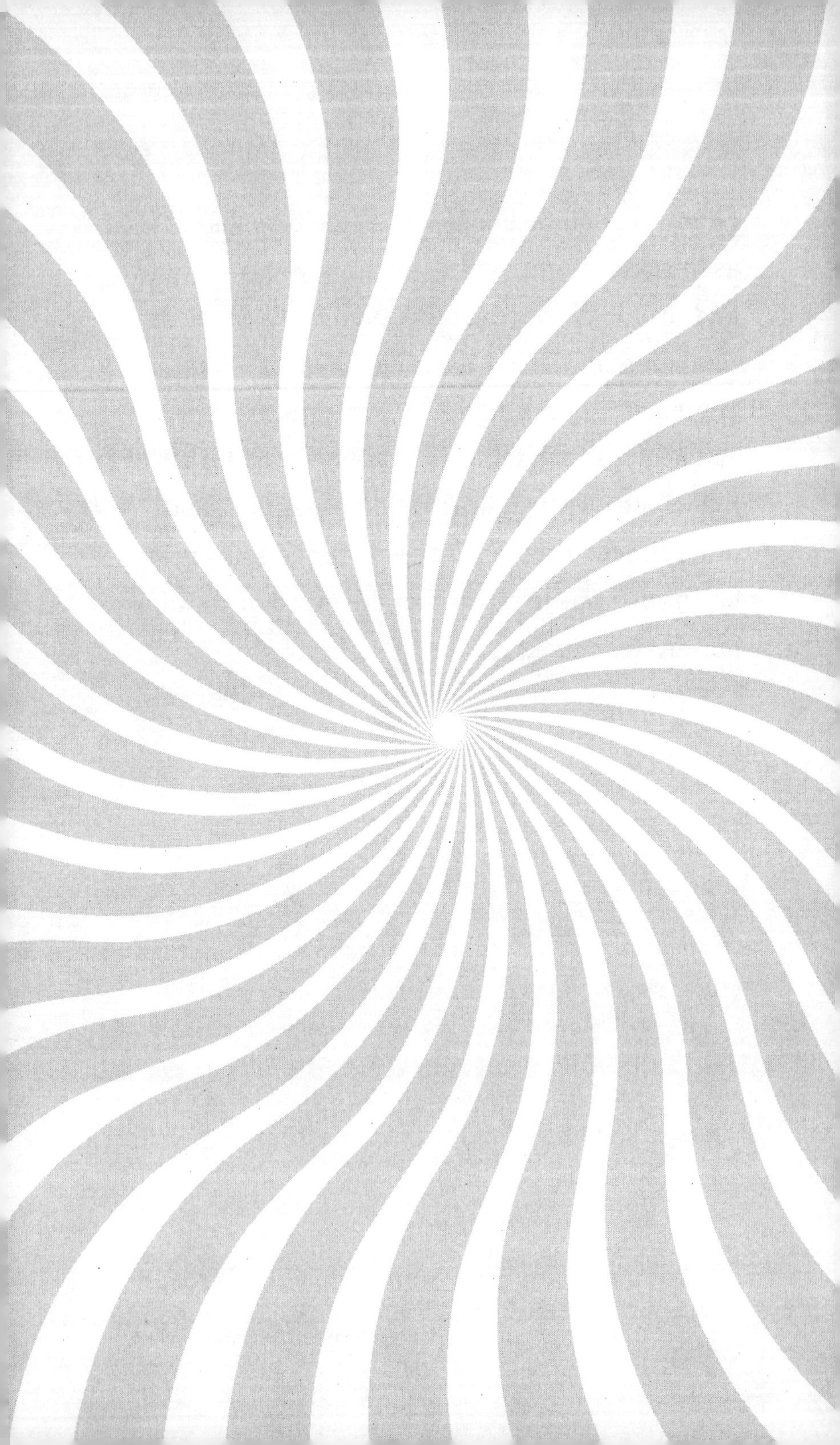

A Note for the Adults in Your Life

In both my professional and personal lives, I have been thinking about social power for years. I am the mother of two boys, and I remember when my oldest, Isaac, came home one day in first grade and told me about how this boy, Dean, who he really admired, purposely excluded him from playing with him and their friend George. In front of Isaac, Dean looked at George and said, "We're not going to let Isaac play with us anymore because he is mean." Knowing that Isaac was quite far from a mean kid, I gave him a lesson on social power. We role played repeatedly how to handle the situation from a social power perspective, how to take back the control and confidently assert himself. He did everything we practiced, and during recess, when Dean reiterated the same thing, Isaac stood right between Dean and George, completely facing George and said, "George, Dean is the mean one. If he keeps this up, we won't let *him* play with *us*." Dean immediately shifted and said, "Wait, we can all play together!" And that was the end of the social power attempts by Dean. It all happened in a fortunate way—Isaac was expressive and shared everything, I happened to be a child psychologist, and my husband appreciated the strategy and participated in the role plays. For many kids, these dynamics go on for a while before getting dealt with, and this can create wounds to their self-esteem, anxiety, and sometimes acting-out behaviors. The complexity of these social power dynamics grows as our children get older. Of all the ages I work with, I find that this issue presents itself most dramatically during the middle-school years.

Social power dynamics occur with both friendships and non-friend peers, and it is when someone tries to have power over your child by either minimizing, ignoring, putting down, excluding, or insulting them. It can be very painful for your child (and for you) to have to confront this, and if it is not dealt with directly, these patterns can persist. It falls on your child to assert themselves and challenge the dynamic. You cannot do it for them, even if you want to (this means you cannot call the parents of other children to try to work it out).

This book is here to help you and your middle-schooler navigate social power with confidence and grace. It is my goal to offer a clear explanation of social power and specific strategies for what to do when it is unequal. The skills required for this task are skills that will contribute greatly to your tween/teen's identity development: skills such as assertiveness, self-confidence, internal locus of control, and being proactive, which will also support your child to become a successful, resilient adult.

Your support of and cheering for your tween or teen is invaluable. Often, it's our parents' voice that we hear in our heads, telling us how worthy we are, and how important and treasured we are. If that voice is critical or harsh, it needs to be corrected. Giving positive messages to support their worth is one of the best things a parent can do, especially during these exciting yet fragile middle-school years. Cheering your child on, having confidence that they can do it, and providing practical support using the messages and strategies outlined here in this book, is the recipe for success.

Sincerely,
Bonnie Zucker, PsyD

Chapter 1

Social Power Defined

Maya was a kind and fun girl who had two best friends, Ashley and Taisha, for most of elementary school. The three of them always hung out together, biking and roller-blading around the neighborhood, and spent most nights texting together. Once they started middle school, things began to shift a bit. They became friends with two other girls, Sasha and Lila, and ate lunch with them every day. The five of them initially hit it off, and it felt like a step up into maturity for Maya, as she was now part of a larger group.

After a few months though, one of the new girls, Sasha, started to have an attitude with Maya. On a few occasions, she made what felt like negative comments to Maya about her appearance; for example, she asked where Maya got her shoes without smiling or saying anything nice about them, and another time, she said something about how Maya "tried too hard" when dressing for school.

Maya

Sasha

She didn't make these comments to Ashley or Taisha. It started out as subtle, little personal jabs, then one day after school, Sasha invited Ashely and Taisha over to her house. They made a TikTok together and took a photo which Sasha posted to her Instagram. Maya felt a pang of uneasiness when she saw the posts, and suddenly she felt like her two best friends weren't just hers anymore.

Has anything like that happened to you?

Jay was an all-around great kid. He liked school and had several close friends but came across as a

| Jay | Ollie | Logan |

little shy. Outside of school, he played on a soccer team which met for three practices and one game a week. Two of the other boys on the team, Ollie and Logan, were more of the competitive type and regularly put Jay down.

If he missed a shot, they would whisper *"loser"* or *"you suck"* to him, or purposely kick the ball at him. Jay watched them looking at him and laughing, and whether the team won or lost, they always had something to say to put down Jay's performance.

Jay found himself less excited about soccer and also noticed that he wasn't playing as well or taking as many risky shots. He thought about saying something but didn't want to ask them to stop, and didn't want to say anything to the coach, because he figured it would only make it worse.

Social Power Defined • 17

So why I am describing these uncomfortable situations? After all, Maya and Jay are amazing kids. Neither of them did anything wrong, and neither of them are to blame for what they were dealing with. They were just going about their business, enjoying their lives, when someone (or in Jay's case, two others) decided to exclude them and put them down. Suddenly, they found themselves in the middle of a social power dynamic.

What is social power, you ask?

In a sense, **social power** is kind of a power trip. It's the power of being the boss or trying to be in charge of kids your age. Sasha, Ollie, and Logan were trying to have power over Maya and Jay. Even though Sasha put Maya down and was excluding her, and Ollie and Logan definitely mistreated Jay, they weren't necessarily bad kids. They were likely still figuring themselves out and still had a lot to learn. Experimenting with social power can be thought of as normal part of growing up, though thinking about it this way doesn't make it any easier for you to deal with!

Social power describes a dynamic between you and another person (of a similar age). When it's unbalanced—when the other person tries to have power over you or take your power away—the power shift can be mild or severe or somewhere in the middle. On the **MILD** side, someone can exclude you, ignore you, be dismissive of you, or talk over you. Basically, they don't respect your importance or belonging to a group. In the **MIDDLE** of the spectrum is when someone puts you down, insults you, or criticizes you.

On the **SEVERE OR EXTREME** side someone may intimidate you, straight up bully you (verbally or even physically) or take your property. In all of these cases, another person is trying to minimize you or make you have less power in the relationship, while making themselves the one with more power and more control. When someone tries to have power over you, they are acting like the authority and giving themselves permission to treat you that way. But just because they give themselves permission to act this way doesn't mean you need to, or should, accept it.

POWER

EQUAL POWER

- Mutual respect
- Mutual generosity
- Easier to be yourself
- Easier to relax & have fun
- Fosters more creativity

DYNAMICS

UNEQUAL POWER

- No mutual respect
- No mutual generosity
- Harder to be yourself
- Interferes with relaxed fun
- Limits creative energy

UNEQUAL POWER

A BULLY IS A PERSON WHO HABITUALLY SEEKS TO HARM OR INTIMIDATE OTHERS, PARTICULARLY KIDS THEY SEE AS VULNERABLE.

Most kids, at some point, try to manage situations or friendship by using social power. Sometimes they do it to make themselves feel better or because they feel insecure. Most of the time it happens without them even knowing they're doing it.

Sometimes one person starts it and the other friend gets caught up in it and ends up participating in the power trip. Regardless of why it happens, social power issues become something you have to deal with. Even though they weren't the cause of their problems, Maya and Jay had to deal with it, and **THEY HAD TO BE THE ONES TO SOLVE IT.**

The dynamics of social power come up both in friendships and with those who are not your friends—or even others who don't know you. The approach to dealing with it will be very different if it's with a friend or with someone who is not a friend. Either way, you need an approach, and the sooner you respond to others trying to have power over you, the better. It starts with a complete understanding of what social power looks like, and what it really means.

YOU CAN SOLVE YOUR SOCIAL POWER STRUGGLES.

Parents, teachers, and coaches might do a great job teaching you about feelings and how to handle them, and you may have heard about ways to deal with stress or frustrations, or learned ways to relax and be mindful, or maybe even tips on how to be more organized in your school work. BUT ... you may have not had a lesson on social power until now.

FOR ADVICE ON HOW TO DEAL WITH STRESS, TO BE MINDFUL AND RELAXED, AND TO GET ORGANIZED IN SCHOOL, CHECK OUT THE OTHER BOOKS IN THIS SERIES!

LET'S START WITH THE BASICS. Power in a relationship is either equal or unequal. When it's equal, there is **MUTUAL RESPECT** and **MUTUAL GENEROSITY**, meaning that both people respect each other as people, including their feelings, preferences, opinions, and qualities, and that both people are interested in giving to each other, try to be fair, take turns, and so on. When the power is equal, your basic rights tend to be protected. When it's unequal, there is a lack of mutual respect and a lack of generosity; for example, someone may look down on you for your opinions, not consider your preferences, and insist on doing things their way without much consideration for how you feel. When the power is unequal, your basic rights are often violated.

JUST LIKE THE GOLDEN RULE (DO UNTO OTHERS AS YOU WOULD HAVE THEM DO UNTO YOU), IT'S ALL ABOUT MUTUAL RESPECT AND MUTUAL GENEROSITY!

The same is true with others who aren't your friends when it comes to respect and generosity. When a classmate who you don't know and are not friends with treats you appropriately, they are showing basic respect. When you are both headed to the desk to pick up a handout at the same time and they give you one first, they are showing respect and generosity.

Many kids are nice, polite, and respectful to those around them. Some kids are indifferent, and they just get the handout and go back to their seat, and that is a neutral move and totally fine. But when someone cuts in front of you or gives you a bad look for no reason, they are putting themselves above you in terms of power by being judgmental and looking down at you. By doing nothing, like Maya and Jay, you will find yourself in an **UNEQUAL SOCIAL POWER DYNAMIC**, just because someone put you down. This is a social power issue.

Once someone does something to have power over you, it immediately creates an unequal, lopsided dynamic (with them on top and you on the bottom). You then have to stick up for yourself and correct this dynamic; by being assertive, you challenge their power and get on their level. When you do this, you make the power equal. Sometimes it may be that you over-correct it and assert yourself over them, giving you more power and making it unequal in your favor. Putting *them* down for putting you down can be an effective temporary move to take back your power so that it ultimately

EQUAL

MUTUAL RESPECT:

> I love the show Wanda Vision.

> Really? I watched and it kinda creeped me out.

> Yeah, I could see that. Soooo many weird parts.

> Totally. But it's a really creative show.

POWER

MUTUAL GENEROSITY:

> I really want pizza.

> OK, but I might get a sub.

> Well, I'm fine with a sub, too.

> Let's get both! Dad, can you please order pizza for Sasha and a sub for me?

UNEQUAL

LACK OF MUTUAL RESPECT:

> I love the show Wanda Vision.

> What?! It's a terrible show! You should watch The Mandalorian instead.

> I think both have a big fan base.

> Whatever. Your show is trash.

POWER

LACK OF MUTUAL GENEROSITY:

> I'm really in the mood for pizza.

> Well, we're getting subs.

> Ok, I guess.

> Subs are better anyway.

re-balances. This isn't my usual advice for teens when it comes to their social life...except when it comes to learning how to play the game of social power. Generally, being kind, respectful, helpful, and well mannered are better ways to act, and I imagine that's the way you try to be. But there is a time to be assertive, for sure!

STICK UP FOR YOURSELF. CHALLENGE THEIR POWER! THAT MEANS YOU'RE ASSERTIVE!

STICK UP FOR YOURSELF! BE ASSERTIVE!

30 • Kid Confident

When it comes to someone purposely trying to put you down, you need to be able to defend yourself emotionally. It's awful how some kids treat others so badly, with disrespect and unkindness, making fun of or shaming them, and feel entitled to do so, yet the one who is receiving this treatment feels uncomfortable talking back and putting them in their place.

Often, it's the nicest kids who struggle with this. **BEING WILLING TO STICK UP FOR YOURSELF AND TALK BACK WITH FIRMNESS MIGHT BE OUTSIDE OF YOUR COMFORT ZONE.** It takes practice. But if you're willing be brave and assert yourself, you'll send the important message.

IF SOMEONE MESSES WITH YOU AND PUTS YOU DOWN, DON'T BACK DOWN AND SHY AWAY; ADVOCATE FOR YOURSELF AND BE THE ONE TO PROTECT YOURSELF.

We will discuss this more in the next chapter on assertiveness, but kids are often worried about coming across as mean when they stick up for themselves (and remember how ironic it is that this isn't something that the one who is trying to have power over you ever worries about!). You will not respond with aggression; the goal is to be appropriately assertive.

DON'T WORRY ABOUT COMING ACROSS AS MEAN. YOU'RE NOT!

Parents and counselors used to give the wrong advice—just ignore it or walk away. This is not effective! When you ignore it and don't stand up and challenge it, the dynamic of unequal power stays exactly the same. **NOTHING AUTOMATICALLY CHANGES!** In addition, when it comes to someone purposely bullying you, your non-response (by ignoring or walking away silently) may be what they are looking for—it may actually give them more power as it shows that they are affecting you!

LOL. JUST IGNORE IT... RIGHT.

This advice of doing nothing, walking away, and ignoring it, in addition to not working, also doesn't teach you the value of sticking up for yourself and your rights. Sticking up for yourself and being assertive is a necessary skill for high school and later into adulthood. So now's the time to learn it!

You have the right to go to school and be treated appropriately by others; Maya had the right to be around her friends without feeling targeted or like her feelings didn't matter; Jay had the right to play soccer without being called names. Although it's not your fault that you have to deal with this problem, you are the only one who can deal with it and change the dynamic.

ASSERTIVENESS IS A NECESSITY FOR ADULTHOOD (AND THE TEEN YEARS, TOO).

Whether it just started happening recently, or has been going on for years, you can do something about it! You can learn the skills of being assertive and responding with confidence. You can practice exactly what to say and how to get it to feel natural and automatic.

Wikipedia is not my usual go-to for information, but its definition of social power is pretty darn good:

> Power is the capacity of an individual to influence the actions, beliefs, or conduct (behavior) of others. The term "authority" is often used for power perceived as legitimate by the social structure.

What does this mean?

It's the part about **"POWER PERCEIVED AS LEGITIMATE"** that stands out. Essentially, if you don't see someone's attempts at having power over you as legitimate or important, then it becomes less relevant and weakens their attempts.

In other words, you can make someone's attempts at having power over you meaningless, mainly by challenging it and not taking it seriously. Then their power play won't work. That is the goal.

For the rest of this book, you will see exactly what goes into a quality friendship and what equal power looks like in friendships, and how to deal when things become unequal. **POWER UPS AND DOWNS ARE COMMON IN FRIENDSHIPS,** but too much imbalance can be a sign that the friendship isn't healthy. Even with best friends, some joking and teasing can be part of your friendship, without compromising the respect you give each other. But you have certain rights in all relationships that must be protected. More about that in the next chapter.

Some social power dynamics are problematic and some are not, and the defining characteristic of each has a lot to do with how it makes you feel. Therefore, **BEING TUNED IN TO YOUR EXPERIENCE AND NOT DISMISSING YOUR FEELINGS IS ESSENTIAL.**

When is Social Power

Social power is unbalanced and unequal when your friend or classmate...

- ○ excludes you,
- ○ ignores you,
- ○ dismisses you or what you have to say,
- ○ puts you down,
- ○ criticizes you,
- ○ insults you,
- ○ laughs at you,
- ○ calls you names,
- ○ tries to get others to reject you or not like you, or
- ○ bullies you (threatens, tries to harm you, harms you, tries to intimidate you)

...to make themselves have more power or control in the relationship, to be in charge, appear as the authority.

⬇

This leads to you feeling bad, embarassed or humuliated, disempowered, vulnerable, or hopeless.

Unequal or Equal?

Social power is fair and equal when your friend or classmate...

- ○ jokes around with you in a fun, mutual way.
- ○ lovingly makes fun of you on occasion and you can freely do the same.
- ○ laughs at you, with you, but stops immediately and apologizes if you show you are upset.
- ○ insults you in a playful manner, in the context of a trusting friendship.
- ○ gently teases you for having a romantic interest, but stops if you get upset.

This is part of a friendship or peer relationship that has good intentions or is playful, and maintains equal power.

⬇

This leads you to laugh, feel closer to the person, and maybe feel a little embarassed but not hurt.

While most kids reading this book are dealing with power imbalances and learning to challenge unequal power dynamics, it's also possible that you might be the power-grabber. If you discover that you are doing this, the first things you can work on to change your power patterns are building more empathy and perspective-taking skills, becoming more self-confident, and growing your emotional intelligence.

Have you heard the expression "walk a mile in someone else's shoes"?

When you show **EMPATHY**, you take the **PERSPECTIVE** of someone else: what is it like to be them in that situation? What would it feel like if you heard that being said to you? What if someone was treating you like that? The more practice you do, the better you will get at it, and the more **CONFIDENT** and **EMOTIONALLY INTELLIGENT** you will become. Emotional intelligence is not the same as book smarts—it has to do with your ability to read others' emotions and understand emotional communication. And people with confidence have little to prove:

- they don't need to put others down to make themselves look better or shine,
- they already believe in themselves,
- they know what they are capable of, and
- they have the ability to make things happen.

True radiance comes from you, not from you in comparison to others. The focus needs to be on lifting up those around you, not putting them down. Being attuned to the subtle parts of how others will make you even more confident in yourself; connecting with others in a real way is a gift and an amazing quality to have in life.

BALANCE THE POWER AND CHANGE YOUR BEHAVIOR WITH EMPATHY, PERSPECTIVE-TAKING, SELF-CONFIDENCE, AND EMOTIONAL INTELLIGENCE.

Grab a pen!

Take a moment and think about a friend with whom you have equal power. You know, that friend who really makes you feel secure and who doesn't try to have power over you. What does this friend do that makes you feel comfortable and like you can just be yourself? What are ways that you both show mutual respect for one another?

HEARD OF "THROUGH THICK AND THIN"? THAT MEANS GOOD FRIENDS SUPPORT EACH OTHER AND HELP EACH OTHER THROUGH GOOD AND BAD TIMES, NO MATTER HOW DIFFICULT THINGS ARE.

Take-Away!

Social power is a dynamic between two peers. When it is balanced and equal, there is mutual respect and generosity. This is important for healthy relationships! When social power is imbalanced or unequal, there is no mutual respect or generosity, and it is harder to be yourself, have fun, and relax. Assertiveness is necessary to fix an unequal social power dynamic! You now have a great overview of social power. It will be helpful as you read the next several chapters to have a few people in mind, examples of others in your own life that you have social power issues with: perhaps make a note of who those people are, and then you can think of those personal examples as you learn the strategies.

Chapter 2

Know Your Rights & Be Assertive

Friendships are an amazing part of life. During middle school and high school (and beyond!), friends contribute so much to your experiences. When you have trusting, supportive friends, you have an extra layer of protection against the ups and downs of life. **SOLID FRIENDSHIPS HELP YOU MAKE BETTER DECISIONS.** Friends help you grow up and help shape you into who you will become. They give you someone to talk to and let you know that someone has your back. Friendships make it possible to socialize and do new and exciting things. Meaningful friendships are to be treasured and nurtured.

When it comes to friends, you may not always think about your rights or the qualities of friendships that matter the most or help you have the best possible relationships. But it makes sense to think about this, especially while you're in middle school and as your friend group expands. As you get older, it's super important to make sure that your relationships are good ones and that you are able to be yourself with your friends. It's crucial to feel accepted and valued by your friends.

Your Rights in Friendships

- To be treated as equal
- To be respected
- To be able to suggest activities
- To be able to decline activities
- For what you say in confidence to be kept private
- To communicate openly and honestly
- To be able to share your feelings without judgment

DECIDING TOGETHER

"Do you want to hang out at your house?"

"Sounds good. We can watch a movie."

"Great!"

EXPRESSING PREFERENCES

"Do you want to watch Star Wars again?"

"Maybe, but we just watched that. How about Hugo Cabret or something else?"

"Sure, totally good. I love Hugo Cabret."

SHARING FEELINGS

"My sister is so immature, it's making my parents fight and it's really hard to be home."

"That's so annoying. I'm sorry."

"Sometimes my brother makes me so angry too."

Qualities of a Good Friendship

- Mutual respect
- Mutual generosity, reciprocated
- Enjoy fun times together, share connection
- Show empathy and understanding toward each other
- Loyal (keep secrets, no gossiping)
- Offer support and guidance when you have a problem to deal with
- Trustworthy and dependable
- Can ask for help or a favor
- Excited when good things happen to you

MUTUAL GENEROSITY

HAVING FUN TOGETHER

STANDING UP FOR EACH OTHER

Directions:

Think about one of your closest friends and take the following quiz to check the quality of your friendship. You can complete the quiz for as many of your friends as you like. For extra fun, you might even consider doing it from your friends point of view to see how you'd match up for them!

1. Do you feel that your friend respects you? Do they listen to you when you have something to say? Are your opinions considered important? If you are upset, does your friend show that they care?

   - A. All of the time
   - B. Some of the time
   - C. Rarely

2. Do you and your friend show generosity with each other, meaning that you give to them and they give to you? Are you both in the habit of doing nice things for each other and showing that you are thinking of each other?

   - A. All of the time
   - B. Some of the time
   - C. Rarely

3. Do you and your friend have fun together and have things in common? Do you find yourself looking forward to getting together with them?

- A. All of the time
- B. Some of the time
- C. Rarely

4. Does your friend seek to understand you and your perspective? When you share your feelings or something that's on your mind, do they show that they care and try to help you feel understood or feel better?

- A. All of the time
- B. Some of the time
- C. Rarely

5. If someone puts you down or trashes you in some way, would your friend stick up for you and defend you? Do you feel that your friend is protective of you?

- A. All of the time
- B. Some of the time
- C. Rarely

6. Is your friend loyal (would never talk about you behind your back)? Does your friend include you in plans with others?

- A. All of the time
- B. Some of the time
- C. Rarely

7. Is your friend someone you could go to for advice? Would they be supportive or offer suggestions on how to solve a problem that you have?

- A. All of the time
- B. Some of the time
- C. Rarely

8. Is your friend trustworthy? Can you tell them your secrets, and know that they will keep it between the two of you? Can you depend on your friend to be there for you if you needed something, like emotional support?

- A. All of the time
- B. Some of the time
- C. Rarely

9. Can you comfortably ask your friend for help or for a favor?

- **A.** All of the time
- **B.** Some of the time
- **C.** Rarely

10. Is your friend happy or excited when good things happen to you? Does your friend cheer you on, without getting jealous?

- **A.** All of the time
- **B.** Some of the time
- **C.** Rarely

Give yourself 3 points for every "A" response, 2 points for every "B" response, and 1 point for every "C" response. Your score will range from 10-30.

25-30 points: HIGH QUALITY friendship: You and your friend have mutual respect, mutual generosity, and seek to understand and support each other. You have fun together, are loyal, and are there for each other if one of you needs help or guidance.

16-24 points: MEDIUM QUALITY friendship: You and your friend have a foundation of good qualities in your relationship, but there is room to grow. Consider which answers were B or C and try to work on those aspects of your relationship. With the right mindset, it can improve!

10-15 points: LOW QUALITY friendship: You and your friend seem to be lacking in many of the qualities that make a friendship meaningful and worthwhile. It may be time to focus your energies on other friendships. Finding friends that you can count on and that really care about you is the goal.

Being treated equally is one of the most important rights in friendship and obviously relates a lot to the topic of this book, but there are other rights that you have in friendships.

When thinking about your friends right now, what qualities are a part of those relationships? Are some friends better at supporting you than others? Are some more sensitive and attuned to you? Are others more fun? What about friendships that are not so positive or ones that don't bring out the best in you?

YOUR GROUP OF FRIENDS WILL PROBABLY CHANGE AND SHIFT DURING THE MIDDLE SCHOOL YEARS.

Many people keep their same friends, but you might want to expand your friend group. Meet new kids. Or you might realize that some of your friendships aren't the best for you at this time in your life. Perhaps you don't have the same interests, don't have as much in common, and don't have as much fun as you used to with certain friends. That's OK. Or maybe you've noticed traits and characteristics that you don't like. What if you realize your friend is judgmental and talks badly about others? Or maybe your friend is super competitive with you, gets jealous, makes negative comments, or puts you down? Maybe you don't want to be part of that friendship anymore.

When a friend makes you feel badly about yourself or puts you in a position where you can't be yourself, that feels awful. If you feel unsure how much you are valued and appreciated by your friend, you may need to do something about it. Often, having an open conversation is the best first step; this can be hard to do or feel awkward, and you may worry about how you will come across, but good friendships should involve the freedom to talk about things openly.

THE STRONGEST AND BEST FRIENDSHIPS ARE THE ONES THAT ARE CONSTANTLY EVOLVING AND GROWING.

If a friend can't grow with you, acts super defensively, or makes you feel badly about yourself for trying to make things better, it may be time to move on! That friendship may no longer be worth your time.

A GOOD FRIENDSHIP INVOLVES TALKING ABOUT THINGS OPENLY.

When you are growing up, you naturally learn about boundaries—those agreed-upon edges or guidelines that exist between people and define how you interact with each other. Boundaries give you the limits of what's expected and what's possible. You wouldn't greet a teacher in the same way you'd greet a friend, because there are boundaries between you and authority figures that guide your behavior.

WITH HEALTHY FRIENDSHIPS, THERE ARE GOOD BOUNDARIES.

You don't insist that your friends do things your way and make them do something they don't want to do. Instead, you have a boundary in place and you respect their personal preferences and ability to decide for themselves. I can go on and on about boundaries, but instead I'll sum it up with this: if you feel uncomfortable or like your feelings, preferences, and wishes don't matter that much to your friend, or if you have an uneasy or unsatisfied feeling about spending time with a friend, take a moment to think about how good or well-defined the boundaries are between you and them. This can help you decide if a friendship is worthwhile or not.

A GOOD BOUNDARY MEANS RESPECTING PERSONAL PREFERENCES AND THE ABILITY TO MAKE YOUR OWN DECISIONS (EVEN WHEN IT MIGHT BE DIFFERENT FROM YOUR FRIENDS').

You may find yourself on the other side of this at times, where someone decides to not be your friend and distances themselves from you. Your friend may decide to shift away from you and hang out with other classmates or the new kid on your team. While this can be hurtful and upsetting, everyone experiences this. It may also be very surprising, and something you weren't expecting, which makes it feel even harder. Once someone has clearly decided they don't want to be friends, it's your job to respect their decision and move on. The more gracefully you handle it, the better. I promise. There is no need to bad-mouth or say anything about your ex-friend;

when you handle it with grace, you preserve your self-esteem.

YOU WILL ALWAYS HAVE SOMETHING VALUABLE THAT YOU OFFER AS A FRIEND, AND YOU MUST KNOW THAT AND HONOR IT.

So, if someone doesn't see your friendship as special, then it's better to put effort into other friendships. When you have **SELF-RESPECT**, it influences how others view you.

What about your rights when it comes to your peers—people your own age who you may not be friends with, or may not even know? Again, you should expect to be treated with respect, especially as you are respectful to others. If you find someone trying to have social power over you, it's up to you to manage it…and that is what you are learning here in this book! ☺

YOU SHOULD EXPECT TO BE TREATED WITH RESPECT AND YOU SHOULD BE RESPECTFUL TO OTHERS.

Going back to social power, the goal is to have mutual respect and mutual generosity. When this doesn't happen, you need to stick up for yourself. In general, others are informed by you in terms of how you expect to be treated. If someone is mean to you and you don't say anything, you are basically telling them that you are willing to tolerate being treated in a mean way.

You are never to be blamed if someone mistreats you! It's not your fault. But your response matters. When you react in an assertive way—where you stick up for yourself with confidence, unapologetically—you are letting others know that you know your worth and your rights and that you won't accept being treated badly.

Remember: **DON'T FOLLOW THE OLD ADVICE OF IGNORING IT AND WALKING AWAY.** If you do nothing, it keeps the power dynamic as it is. If someone is putting you down to lift themselves up, and you leave it unchallenged, nothing will change (and it may even get worse over time!).

YOU ARE NOT TO BLAME IF SOMEONE MISTREATS YOU.

If someone mistreats you, don't respond by screaming, cursing, fighting, or being physical in any way. If you do that, you've totally lost control and that could strengthen the other person's power (especially if they laugh at you while you unleash!). The goal is to be assertive but calm.

What Is Assertiveness?

ASSERTIVENESS is basically being able to stand up for yourself or for others, without being passive or aggressive. It's a power skill that will benefit you a million times over throughout your life. There is a range to being assertive. Sometimes you just need to say something subtly or slide a comment in to let the other person know that you are confident and won't take being pushed around. Other times, it's more direct and requires a bigger step on your part to really stand up to someone. When it comes to more direct assertiveness, it's really useful to practice the situation in advance until responding assertively comes more naturally to you. Since it's a skill, **PRACTICE IS NECESSARY.**

Assertiveness comes out in both what you say and how you say it, and also how you stand and look. A powerful message isn't as powerful if it's said in a quiet voice, so tone of voice is important.

Here's how to do it:

1. Talk in a clear, firm voice that is loud enough for others to hear (but not yelling).

2. Stand tall (no slouching), like a mountain.

3. Make eye contact; look them right in the eye (don't look down or away).

Some kids worry about coming across as mean when they are asserting themselves. Many times, talking in an assertive tone with eye contact and saying things to challenge someone's power over you can feel unnatural and scary. **BUT SERIOUSLY.** Being able to be assertive is part of being the best you, your most confident self! Remember: it's on you to let others know that you require respect from them and that you respect yourself. By being your own advocate, you are communicating both messages to others. If someone feels comfortable disrespecting you, you need to get comfortable standing up for yourself and talking back to them, not worrying that you are hurting their feelings or being mean! And it's clear by their behavior that they are not at all worried about doing the same to you!

FOR EXAMPLE!

THE BACKSTORY: Cassidy spent the summer hanging out with one of her closest friends, Mary, and two other girls, Sam and Clara, who went to their school but hadn't really spent time with them before that summer. The four got along extremely well all summer long. When school started back, Sam and Clara went back to hanging with their main friend group, and Mary started to distance herself from Cassidy and ended up saying something bad about Cassidy, making fun of her for something from over the summer.

THE SOCIAL POWER FIX: Cassidy texted Mary:

> "I think you might have forgotten that we just had the best summer together. I know you've been talking about me. I'm not sure what's up, but that's so not you! I am bummed that this is who you've become."

Mary texted right back with an honest apology and told Cassidy that she felt badly after she did that. Cassidy then softened and texted back:

> Thank you for owning up to it, that really means a lot to me. ♡♡

THE RESULT: And that was that. Cassidy was really proud of herself and Mary did a wonderful job immediately respecting Cassidy and re-balancing the power. Even though this was over text, it's still easy to see that Cassidy was clear and direct and firm in the way she was talking to Mary.

FOR EXAMPLE!

THE BACKSTORY: Xander was riding the bus to school when an older kid, Austin, started to give him a hard time. First, he made a comment about Xander's backpack, then he asked him about what model phone he had and made some mean jokes, and then he teased him for his "bad haircut." This went on for almost two weeks, until Xander didn't want to take the bus anymore. Even though it was difficult, Xander understood:

- he can't allow his fears to influence his decisions, and
- he had to take this as an opportunity to practice social power dynamics.

THE SOCIAL POWER FIX: So he made a plan. Xander figured out what to say and practiced role-playing a few times (more about why role plays are helpful in Chapter 7).

He even made a video of him role-playing so he could listen back for extra practice before he rode the bus again. If the plan didn't work, he'd talk to the school transportation director (normally I don't suggest this, but Xander needed to know he had a Plan B if challenging the power didn't work).

THE RESULT: Xander went back on the bus the next morning, and when the kid came on and sat across from him, unlike the past times, Xander looked right at him and the kid said "What?" in a rude tone, and Xander said, "Nothing" with a tone of confidence, clear and firm voice, sitting up straight, maintaining eye contact. The kid then made a comment about his backpack again and Xander said, "Stop talking to me and stop sitting near me and get over yourself." The kid then said "I guess backpack boy has an attitude" and then that was it! Xander then put his earphones on and looked out the window. The kid never said anything to Xander again.

These two examples had really good outcomes. They were relatively easy to deal with and give you a clear idea of what assertiveness looks and feels like. But what happens if things don't work this easily? Or what if they escalate? This will be discussed in much greater detail (in Chapter 4) but for now, know that safety comes first in all cases. What you've been reading relates to situations where you are managing social power imbalances within a safe context. BUT if you ever feel threatened or like someone could hurt you, then this goes beyond a social power problem and more into a bullying situation. In those situations, do not hesitate to involve teachers, adults, or school counselors. Your safety is **THE MOST** important thing and matters above all else.

IF YOU ARE BEING THREATENED, DO WHATEVER IT TAKES TO STAY SAFE.

Get away from the situation, even if it means that you get embarrassed or literally have to run away. Definitely tell a parent or another trusted adult if this happens, not just because it's scary and you need some support, but because they will help you decide how to best handle it.

Here's something you should know about since it's such an important part of being happy and successful in life—an **internal locus of control**. When you have an internal locus of control, you believe that there is something that you can do to either change a situation or affect your experience of it. The opposite is an **external locus of control**, which is when you think it doesn't matter what you do, and that the situation is what it is and it's out of your control. People with an internal locus of control are better at problem-solving in situations because they focus on what they can do, what they can change, or try, and so on. They also don't give up as easily because they focus on their own efforts.

YOU'RE NOT HELPLESS! YOU HAVE CONTROL. YOU CAN RELY ON YOU.

The Studies Show...

- 7,500 adults from the UK were studied over 20 years! The study found that those who had an internal locus of control at age 10 were less likely to be overweight at age 30. So they were at lower risk of obesity. They also reported better health and less stress.

- Another study showed that people with an internal locus of control saved more money, in case they needed it later on.

- Another study showed that those who had an internal locus of control spent more time and effort searching for a job when they were unemployed.

INTERNAL Locus of Control vs.

INTERNAL Locus of Control

- Believe that you can change or influence a situation
- Focus on your responsibility in a situation
- Strong sense of self-efficacy; work hard toward goals
- Focus on problem-solving and finding creative solutions
- More likely to feel empowered and optimistic

EXTERNAL Locus of Control

- Believe that situations are out of your control and there's nothing you can do to change it
- Blame others or outside factors for situation
- Tend to give up more easily
- More likely to feel helpless or experience depression

EXTERNAL Locus of Control

SITUATION:

"I have no friends at my new school."

RESPONSE WITH AN INTERNAL LOCUS OF CONTROL:

- ☐ Think of ways to meet others
- ☐ Join others at lunch
- ☐ Sign up for clubs
- ☐ Talk to school counselor about sitting at lunch with other students

RESPONSE WITH AN EXTERNAL LOCUS OF CONTROL:

- ☐ Complain, cry to parents
- ☐ Think about switching schools
- ☐ Blame other kids for not being outgoing or welcoming
- ☐ Feel disempowered and discouraged

The reason that internal locus of control is so important at your age is because this is also the time in your childhood journey—during your adolescence—where you develop a sense of personal agency.

Personal agency is your ability to rely on yourself to get things done and make things happen for your life. For example, when my son was 10, he got really into photography and his dad helped him set up his own website to post his best photographs for sale. Having his own website of his photos helped to create his sense of personal agency. When you initiate and solve problems on your own, you are showing personal agency; **ASKING FOR HELP AND SUPPORT IS GREAT**—the main thing is that you lead the effort and want to solve the problem.

Personal agency also has a lot to do with **self-efficacy**, which is your belief in yourself to accomplish a certain task. If you have high self-efficacy, you will look at a specific task—maybe it's a project you have for school or a challenging work out you signed up for or even just having to clean your room—and say to yourself, **"I CAN DO THIS. I'VE GOT THIS!"** and then you get to it. Personal agency involves this self-efficacy skill plus an actual skill of being able to do something. When you have both, you're golden!

Why is this important when it comes to social power and managing power in relationships? Well, it's essential that you believe in your ability to do this and know that you can **POWER UP!** It also connects with assertiveness because when you believe that you can stick up for yourself and that it will matter and can make a difference in how things turn out, you will be more likely to do it.

BELIEVE IN YOUR ABILITY TO POWER UP. YOU GOT THIS!

Grab a pen!

Since having an internal locus of control is so important, especially when it comes to creating personal agency, can you think about a tough situation you are dealing with and what you might do to change it? What is within your control? How can you think differently about it?

Personal Agency

PERSONAL AGENCY

- ☐ Your ability to make things happen in your life
- ☐ Relates to self-efficacy, which is your belief in your ability to accomplish specific tasks
- ☐ Relates to your skill to accomplish tasks
- ☐ Impacts the sense of control you have in your life

SITUATION:

"I really want a new PlayStation and my parents say they'll contribute some money but I need to come up with most of it."

RESPONSE WITH PERSONAL AGENCY:

- ☐ Come up with a business to help older adults learn basic computer skills and solve computer issues
- ☐ Advertise at grandparents' retirement community
- ☐ Because of my solid computer skills and ability to explain things clearly, the business is a huge success and I end up buying the new PlayStation on my own

Take-Away!

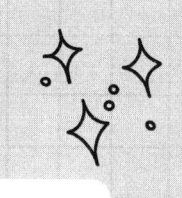

Now you have the basics when it comes to understanding and thinking about friendships, your rights, and what to do if things start to get unequal. Healthy relationships are crucial for a happy and successful life. A good friendship is based on mutual respect and generosity, and includes things like sharing feelings, being able to voice opinions, trusting that your secrets will be kept, and healthy boundaries. Be assertive about your rights in friendships! Also key to a happy and successful life are an internal locus of control (feeling that you can control things in your life), self-efficacy (your belief in your own abilities), and personal agency (your ability to make things happen). To help you along even more, next up, we will focus on self-confidence!

Chapter 3

Discover Self-Confidence & Self-Control

You probably have a decent idea what self-confidence looks like when you think about certain athletes or pop stars, but let's dig a little deeper in what it means for you. **Self-confidence** is a general belief and trust in yourself and your ability to get things done. When you are self-confident, you know your strengths and believe in yourself and that you will be able to accomplish what you set out to do. It's different from **self-esteem**, which is more about your sense of self-worth and a deeper sense of how valuable you feel you are. **IF YOU HAVE STRONG SELF-ESTEEM YOU EXPECT TO BE TREATED WELL AND WILL LIKELY NOT ACCEPT LESS FOR YOURSELF.** It makes sense that the more often you respond to situations in your life with a sense of confidence, the more you develop a greater sense of self-worth, which will strengthen your self-esteem.

SELF-CONFIDENCE IS ABOUT BELIEVING IN YOURSELF!

Self-confidence develops over time, especially as you have more practice with going after a goal and achieving it. This is why it's so important to put yourself out there and take reasonable risks, because you will learn about yourself as you do. Even if you are not totally sure that you will be able to do something at first, when you try and stick with it, often you will find that you can get it done and can do it well! As you do more and more in life, and have the right kind of thinking along the way (this is VERY important and we will discuss thinking errors in a moment, and positive thinking in a later chapter), the more your **CONFIDENCE WILL GROW.**

PUTTING YOURSELF OUT THERE AND TAKING REASONABLE RISKS BUILDS CONFIDENCE!

Of course, another way of building confidence is managing challenging situations in your life, such as social power issues, successfully. Self-confidence allows you to **STAND UP FOR YOURSELF** and your rights; it also develops and strengthens when you do this (meaning that sticking up for yourself when appropriate leads to even more confidence). When you respond with assertiveness, you end up showing confidence. Interestingly, acting confident, even when you don't totally feel confident, makes you more confident!

The Studies Show...

- People who feel self-confident with an internal locus of control have an easier time making decisions.

- Children with strong self-confidence do better at school and are happier at their jobs as adults.

- Athletes who are self-confident perform better, and self-confidence is a skill found in successful top athletes.

- Self-esteem is strongly related to positive mental health.

Here are five ways to do just that. We will talk about these things in this chapter.

1. ACKNOWLEDGE WHAT YOU CAN GIVE.
What do you bring into your friends' life that is positive and meaningful and helpful? Valuing yourself and what you mean to others also grows confidence.

My mom is always mad at me. I'm always down. No one cares.

That's really hard, but remember that I care a lot.

2. DISCOVER YOUR PASSIONS.
There are so many things that you can be good at doing—hobbies, activities, sports, writing, roller-skating, acting whatever. Think about anything that is interesting or exciting to you, and go for it.

3. **TAKE RISKS AND PUT YOURSELF OUT THERE.** Sorry to be repetitive ☺ but this is an important one. Go for what you want. Be guided by your dreams, not your fears. Whatever the outcome, you will not regret giving it a try; reward yourself for your effort.

4. **HAVE SELF-COMPASSION, NOT SELF-CRITICISM.** Self-compassion is when you show kindness to yourself, and give yourself a break when you are having a hard time or not doing something well or not doing it perfectly; it's the ultimate way of supporting and loving yourself! The opposite is self-criticism, which is when you are hard on yourself and say mean or even shaming things to or about yourself. When you are harsh and critical with yourself, you actually make it **HARDER** to reach your goals; people are better able to achieve their goals when they have self-compassion. Don't bring yourself down; instead, lift yourself up with a gentle dose of being compassionate and understanding and kind to yourself. By honoring yourself this way, you are supporting your sense of confidence.

> Ugh! I forgot to finish this English assignment! Ok, let me just get it done now. There's been so much this week, everyone makes mistakes!

5. SHOW SELF-CONTROL, PERSONAL AGENCY, AND SELF-CONFIDENCE. Don't be reactive or aggressive to negative situations, such as when someone is being unkind to you. Instead, keep your composure, which shows that you are in control of yourself. This maturity will be noticed by others and they will think better of you, which also helps you feel more confident.

So, how do you become self-confident? Standing up for your rights and sticking up for yourself when others put you down are big ways to develop it, but there are others!

The mental mindset of confidence is about choosing to **BELIEVE IN YOURSELF**, saying supportive things to yourself about yourself, and taking actions that align with your values and your goals. It's about having self-control (and the confidence to show it). When someone is proactive in these ways, they make decisions based on their values; this is the opposite of being reactive, which is when you make decisions based on your feelings. If you feel nervous about something and avoid it, that is being reactive. If you feel nervous about something and push yourself to do it and face the situation, that is being **PROACTIVE**...and it happens to be the way that you figure out that you can do it, which builds more self-confidence.

PROACTIVE = DECISIONS BASED ON VALUES
REACTIVE = DECISIONS BASED ON FEELINGS

Later on in this book we will focus on thinking and self-talk; self-talk is what you say to yourself and it can be **VERY** powerful! As you are learning about self-confidence now, here's one of the most helpful self-talk messages you can use:

- What would someone who is self-confident think in this situation? What would they do?
- What would someone with strong self-confidence think? What would they do?

The content of these two statements is the same, but wording things a certain way is more helpful to some than others. So you have options! Prompting yourself to think with confidence actually works.

When it comes to self-confident thinking, I'd like to encourage you to have a can-do attitude. Self-confident people **FOCUS ON THEIR GOALS AND GO FOR IT;** their mindset expects things to work out well. When we expect a good outcome, it becomes motivating for us to put the effort in. This is also where your internal locus of control comes in again: when you believe that you can impact a situation or affect how things turn out, you are more likely to take action. Self-confident thinking can also become self-talk.

I've got this!
I can do it!

Things will work
out for me.

There is a lot I
can do to make
this better.

What is within my
control here?

What efforts
can I focus on?

I believe in
myself and am thinking
of my past successes!

Are there other things you can say to yourself to bring about that feel-good energy?

FOR EXAMPLE!

Damien wanted to build his own computer. His parents were supportive of his goal but didn't know anything about computers. He spent hours every weekend watching YouTube tutorials and taking notes, identified all of the necessary components to buy, stuck within the budget, and explained the steps in detail to his parents. Damien believed that he could do it. He then successfully built his own computer! After that, he made a YouTube tutorial of his own for beginners, to show how it was done!

FOR EXAMPLE!

Kimmy had always wanted to try fencing. She asked her mom to look into it for her, and her mom signed her up for a week-long camp for beginners where she discovered her passion for sabre fencing. She didn't know anyone at the camp but made a group of new friends! Although it was a little scary to walk into a camp where she didn't know anyone and try something new, taking that risk proved to be worth it.

FOR EXAMPLE!

George struggled a great deal with math. Most other subjects came fairly easily, and he earned As and Bs in everything except math, where he worked the hardest to get a C. When his report card came out, his parents expressed that they were proud and he joined them and shared that while he doesn't like a C on his report card, he knew that his effort was strong. He showed kindness toward himself.

Damien, Kimmy, and George all felt confident and it guided their thoughts and actions. As you see from these examples, their thoughts affected their feelings and how they responded in each situation. When you focus on positive thoughts, you feel more confident, and then are more willing to take steps toward a goal, or even take some reasonable risks. So, our thoughts, feelings, and actions are all connected and all affect each other.

There's a type of therapy called cognitive-behavioral therapy (CBT for short) where you look at your thinking patterns to figure out what you can switch around to have a better experience. Everyone makes **thinking errors** from time to time; for example, kids who have a lot of anxiety often use catastrophizing, which is when you automatically think of all the bad things that could go wrong and do a lot of what if…worrying. There are other thinking errors that may come up when you are in your middle school years. Let's go through six of the most common ones:

- All-or Nothing
- Mind Reading
- Filtering
- Shoulds
- Personalization
- Selective Attention

THINKING

ALL-OR-NOTHING:

When you think in extremes: it's either perfect or a failure, it's either easy or impossible, with no middle ground.

Example: My friends all hung out together after school without inviting me. I need to find a new friend group.

MIND READING:

When you think you know what others are thinking about you, and it tends to be negative. Without them saying so, you conclude that others don't like you.

Example: I can tell those kids don't think I'm interesting. They'd rather me not be here.

ERRORS

FILTERING:

Focusing on the negatives and ignoring the positives.

Example: James was a jerk today—all he did was give me a hard time. (Yet James's mom texted your mom photos of you and James laughing and having a blast.)

SHOULDS:

When you make rules for yourself and/or others. Rules sound like "I should…" or "Others shouldn't…" and are to show how things should be.

Example: You shouldn't just sit with kids you don't know. You shouldn't think it's okay to just join them without being invited.

...MORE THINKING ERRORS

PERSONALIZATION:

When you take more responsibility than you should for a negative situation. When you make something about you, taking it personally.

Example: Those kids gave me a bad look after practice. I didn't play my best and that's probably why they looked at me like that.

SELECTIVE ATTENTION:

When you have a belief and you only focus on information that confirms it, while ignoring information that goes against it.

Example: Even though all the camps I've done before were new to me and I liked some of them, I won't like trying this new camp. Like that time I tried a drawing class and didn't like it.

When looking at this list, do you know which thinking errors you make?

Take some time to learn about these thinking errors and pick out the ones you find yourself making most often. People tend to make the same thinking errors over and over. If you can take a minute to let them go and find another way of seeing the situation, you can get back on track and face any social power situation that is bugging you.

THINKING ERRORS JUST GET IN THE WAY!

For example, if you are **mind-reading** and think that others don't want you to join them at the bus stop, or think that they don't like you (even though there is no evidence to support that!), you will not try to connect with them. Thinking this way will likely prevent you from talking to them or trying to join their conversation, and by avoiding it, your mind-reading thoughts will only get **EVEN STRONGER.** Or you may stand close by, but stay quiet, and not express yourself confidently. When you are able to see that you are mind-reading, and that thinking this way is actually a thinking error, you will be better able to challenge yourself and think "I don't really know what they are thinking, just like others don't really know what I'm thinking! Someone who felt **CONFIDENT** in this situation would not be having these thoughts and instead would focus on who they wanted to talk to." Then you will just walk up to them and jump in with a question like "can't believe the bus is late again!" or "cool shoes."

SOCIAL COMPETENCE

COMPETENCE means that you are able to do something successfully. If you are competent at something, you have strong knowledge or skill. You can be competent at a certain sport, a musical instrument, or a hobby. You can also be socially competent, meaning that you have strong social skills and a solid ability to manage social relationships and interactions. In thinking about self-confidence, one additional way to build it is to make sure that you have strong social competence.

SOCIAL COMPETENCE IS HAVING STRONG SOCIAL SKILLS & KNOWING HOW TO MANAGE SOCIAL SITUATIONS.

There are many skills that go into being socially competent. A good overall phrase to think of is **BUILD BRIDGES, NOT BARRIERS.** Consider what makes people likeable or sought after; what draws you to them? Then borrow those same qualities to draw people toward you.

BUILDING BRIDGES MAKES PEOPLE FEEL MORE CONNECTED TO YOU, LIKE YOU MORE, AND WANT TO BE AROUND YOU.

Try things like asking people what they like to do, giving them genuine compliments, and being sincerely interested in who they are and what makes them smile **(BE HAPPY).** Sharing about things that you are excited about or recently enjoyed doing, being enthusiastic about good things that happen to others, and showing concern when someone is upset are other bridges that build connections. Even remembering someone's name and using it when talking with them helps build a bridge, as it makes the person feel special. Finally, sticking up for someone is another type of bridge you can build.

BARRIERS, ON THE OTHER HAND, KEEP OTHERS DISTANCED AND MAKE OTHERS WANT TO AVOID US.

Barriers are like a closed door that says **DO NOT ENTER** and are things like being overly competitive, critical, a sore loser, reactive, or aggressive (name calling, putting others down, and so on).

We are all capable of building bridges or barriers; choose bridges! There are lots of ways to build bridges, but listen to what I heard from Peter, a kid who happens to be totally socially competent and can make new friends easily.

I am sure it took him some practice and lots of confidence, but here is how he builds bridges.

THINGS I VALUE IN A FRIEND

- ☐ Always have my back
- ☐ Make me laugh
- ☐ Always are there for me if I have problems with someone or maybe if I need something or just feel sad
- ☐ Talk with me about things I want
- ☐ Treat me with kindness and respect

HOW I CONNECT WITH OTHERS

- ☐ Make them laugh
- ☐ Understand them
- ☐ Get to know them
- ☐ Am nice or friendly
- ☐ Smile
- ☐ Show kindness
- ☐ Am open to ideas and things
- ☐ Lighten up their day
- ☐ Always have their back
- ☐ Am always there for them
- ☐ Willingly talk about what they want
- ☐ Treat them with kindness and respect

Another area of social competence is knowing how to join a group of kids who are socializing or playing together. The best thing to do is to approach these situations with confidence and know how to not give your power away. When you go in with confidence, you are focused on what you want and go for it; if you go in with a sense of doubt, you may begin to question if they want you to join, or if they will like you, or if you are interesting or fun enough. Those self-doubting thoughts will make it harder for you to come across as confident (plus, those doubts keep you in your own head, so it's harder to be engaging).

CONFIDENCE IS ADMIRABLE—IT MAKES OTHERS ADMIRE YOU AND FEEL GOOD BEING AROUND YOU.

If this isn't easy for you, don't worry: with practice and as you keep having the right kind of thoughts, you will get there.

The goal is to **ASSUME YOU CAN JOIN AND ASSUME YOU ARE WELCOMED TO JOIN!** If you ask to join ("Can I sit here?" "Can I come, too?"), you are giving your power away! How is this giving your power away, you ask? Well, if you ASK, then the other person or people now have the power to say "yes" or "no" to you. It then becomes *their* decision so they have control over deciding if they'll allow you to join or not; they hold the power. **DO NOT ASK TO JOIN! DO NOT GIVE YOUR POWER AWAY!** Just join without asking, assume you are included, and then if you hang out for a while and get a sign that you are not wanted (like if the others are not including you in the conversation or ignoring you), then you will take the hint and leave the situation gracefully. Let's run through an example of when it works and what to do when it doesn't.

When it works...

In PE, three girls are in a conversation and you overhear them talking about a show you watch. You naturally make a comment about this season, they acknowledge your comment, keep talking, and make room for you to stand within their circle (non-verbally including you).

And what to do when it doesn't...

You have a new lunch period without any of your friends, so you see a group of boys sitting at a table and decide to sit next to them. They don't acknowledge you, you make a comment and they ignore it. After 15 minutes, you say "Oh, there's someone I want to say hi to" and get up and leave.

> Aren't you in my Spanish class?

REMEMBER: DO NOT ASK TO JOIN! THAT GIVES YOUR POWER AWAY!

A real test to both your self-confidence and your social competence is how well you handle a situation when you are not being included. Like in the illustration on the last page, you saw how the boy was able to naturally disengage while maintaining his confidence.

What happens when, for example, you discover that your friends have been invited to someone's house and you weren't? Or some other friends have signed up for a week-long camp this summer and didn't tell you about it or ask if you would sign up as well? What do you do in these situations, and how do you handle them?

It's hard when you are hurt or feel left out. Painful feelings often turn into anger. Just be careful. It's easy to badmouth others, call them names for not including you, reject them for rejecting you, and so on. This is like reaching for the low hanging fruit—it's easy to grab a hold of but it's often not the best fruit on the tree; it may be harder to climb up to get the better fruit, but the effort is worth the reward.

The same is true in these social situations. Don't react, but instead manage these situations with calmness and grace. Instead of getting mad at the person who didn't invite you but invited all of your friends, could you make other plans for yourself and then the next day confidently ask your friends, "How was last night? Did you have a fun time?"

For the friends who go to the week-long camp, or have some other big planned group activity, can you ask them about it, say something like "wow, that sounds interesting," and then share what you will be doing that week? Can you maintain your confidence and knowledge in how great you are and how you don't need to be included in order to feel valued?

Maybe you would invite your friends for a plan and even include the one who didn't ask you (though I would only do this once or twice, and if I was still not included—if there still wasn't reciprocity—then I wouldn't keep inviting them because this then gives them more social power).

When you act with self-confidence in situations in which you are not included, you are actually making it less of a loss for yourself, because you keep your **SENSE OF PRIDE** and belief in who you are. By being less influenced by the circumstances and holding onto your sense of worth, you come out on top. We will talk more in the next chapter about navigating these situations.

Take-Away!

Self-confidence is an important skill and key in dealing with social power issues. Self-confidence, assertiveness, internal locus of control, and being proactive are all *protective factors* in life, meaning that by developing these skills and thinking and behaving this way, you will have protection against mental health issues such as anxiety and depression. You also learned about thinking errors and decision making and how to work on both. Finally, by focusing on these skills, your self-esteem will improve as well.

Chapter 4

Find Mutual Respect & Generosity

Ideal friendships are defined by both mutual respect and mutual generosity. When these qualities are present, you'll have equal power with your friends and things will generally run smoother in your friend groups. When power is equal, you and your friends will make decisions **TOGETHER** and prioritize making sure that everyone agrees and is happy about the plans. When the relationships are the priority, you will feel supported by your friends and naturally feel closer to them. When the power is equal, no one is trying to control the other person. With equal power, everyone's feelings and everyone's preferences count.

This chapter is going to be all about ideal friendships and social power with your friends or friend group. In the next chapter we will deal with social power issues with non-friends, general peers, and others who you don't know who try to have power over you.

EQUAL POWER MEANS NO ONE TRIES TO CONTROL SOMEONE ELSE.

All of this feels like such a big deal, but keep in mind that in all good friendships, power issues will come up from time to time. That's just reality. Maybe someone feels strongly about something, wants to be right, is having a bad day, or just has a momentary shift of how they treat you. When you have realistic expectations that social power issues will sometimes happen, you are better prepared to maintain your confidence in the friendship and not get too thrown by temporary shifts in social power.

Even your best friends will challenge your power, and you will notice that sometimes a friend acts a certain way, is irritable and takes it out on you, puts you down, or is negative with you or about you. During these times, try to:

- not personalize it (this is about them, not you), and
- stand up for yourself by being assertive.

If you don't take it personally, you are able to respond in a clear, assertive way; if you personalize it, you may react too strongly or aggressively. That might do more harm than good and hurt your friendship—plus, it won't give you an opportunity to practice managing these situations with grace and confidence. (And with friends, it is usually a safe and easy place to practice assertiveness!).

So, what do you do when your friend isn't showing equal power and isn't being respectful to you?

1. **GIVE YOUR FRIEND THE BENEFIT OF THE DOUBT.** By giving them a break here and there when power struggles come up, you're respecting your friend and giving them space to let their feelings out. But if it really bothers you or starts to become a pattern, then you need to do something to challenge and correct it.

2. **DISENGAGE OR PULL BACK TO SHOW HOW YOU FEEL.** When you disengage, you pull back, say less, change the topic or focus of the conversation, or appear to be a bit distant. Becoming distanced is less direct and does not show real assertiveness, but it will often cue a good friend that they are not treating you the right way (an attuned friend will pick up on it) and make them wonder what's wrong.

3. **BE ASSERTIVE.** Be respectful, but clear and confident when you do this. Always stick up for yourself. We will review specific examples on how to do this well.

4. As a last resort, **CALL YOUR FRIEND OUT.** You might even need to say something like, "I'm not sure what's going on for you right now, but it's not cool—you gotta stop." Or "Is something wrong? Did I do something to upset you?"

Many times, your friend may not even realize they are acting that way and testing the power balance. When they do, and especially if it becomes a pattern or they push back, you need to stay firm and not give in to being treated like that, as it minimizes your power. It's so important to protect your sense of power and keep things as equal as possible. For the sake of your own self-worth, let others know that you are valuable and important and not willing to be put down or pushed around.

When a friend isn't showing equal power, try to...

- give your friend the benefit of the doubt.
- disengage or pull back to show how you feel.
- be assertive.
- call your friend out on it directly.

Let's run through three examples of typical social power dynamics that can come up in meaningful friendships and within friend groups and how you might resolve them.

FOR EXAMPLE!

THE BACKSTORY: Josh and his three friends were Facetiming when one of his friends suggested that they add a girl from their class into the group call. Josh said he didn't want to, and one of his friends accused him of liking her and said "I'm going to tell her that you want to go out with her." Josh got very upset and started yelling at his friend for saying this. His friend then kept giving him a hard time, said that he must like her if he cares so much about her joining, and threatened to add her in.

THE SOCIAL POWER FIX: Josh gave his friends several warnings and then decided to hang up and get off the call. He then texted his friends on their group chat:

> Not cool. Going to play Roblox now where I won't get harassed for no reason.

THE RESULT: Josh's friend who started the joke immediately Facetimed him back and apologized. Josh said "it's all good" and they went on to have a normal conversation. Josh was able to hang out with the girl in gym class without his friends harassing him.

FOR EXAMPLE!

THE BACKSTORY: Carly asked to hang out with her friend Zoey after school, and Zoey said she was sorry but she had something she had to do. Carly then found out that Zoey went home with their other friend, Jessica, and purposely didn't include her. Carly also discovered that Zoey and Jessica planned a matching Halloween costume without including Carly.

Carly

THE SOCIAL POWER FIX: Carly confronted Zoey and said "Listen, it's totally fine when one of us hangs out without the other, so next time you don't need to stress or be secretive about it. Anyway, I think your costume is great and I already have my avocado costume which I can't wait to wear. I'm so excited to trick-or-treat together."

THE RESULT: Zoey apologized for being secretive and made a plan to hang out with Carly the next day.

FOR EXAMPLE!

THE BACKSTORY: Len and a group of friends were playing basketball and he wasn't playing his best. Several of his friends started teasing him and giving him a hard time. It went on for much of the time they were playing. By the end, Len's feelings were definitely hurt.

THE SOCIAL POWER FIX: At the end of basketball, Len told his closest friend, "This was completely annoying."

THE RESULT: His friend realized that Len was hurt and said "Yeah, it went too far," and the two of them biked home together and hung out at Len's house. No one gave him a hard time after that.

Josh, Carly, and Len had these upsetting situations that were all social power issues that were coming up in their friendships. What do you think of how they resolved them? How you would handle these situations?

Josh, Carly, and Len stood up for themselves with confidence and assertiveness. For Josh and Len, they made it clear that the way there were being treated was not okay, and without making a huge deal or even saying very much, they expressed themselves effectively. All three situations were resolved well, and their friends rose to the occasion and made things right. It won't always work out like this, and sometimes you won't get the validation you want or you will have to let things lie or wait it out a bit before it gets back to normal. Regardless, the goal is to expect to be treated with respect.

One thing to note about Carly's response that's not always easy to do: Carly wasn't included, yet she didn't take it personally! While it was upsetting that she wasn't included and she did feel like she missed out, she took the high road and validated the quality of her friendship with Zoey. She acted confident, not insecure.

How to Not Take

Don't make it about you!
It's about them and not you.

Remember: Personalization is a thinking error and it's when you take too much responsibility for a negative outcome, or make something about you when it's really not.

Say to yourself...How would someone with strong self-confidence think in this situation? What would they do?

Others' behavior reflects on them, not on you.

Look for explanations of others' actions that have nothing to do with you.

Things Personally

Empathize with the other person, trying to understand their position.

Acknowledge that you're upset, feel left out, etc., and stay mindful to the feelings without wallowing in them.

Remind yourself of your value and think of others who value or include you.

Remember that taking things personally means that you are giving your power away.

Cope well by finding another plan or activity to do.

When you are not naturally included in your friends' plans, you can try a few different things:

1. **JOIN IN.** Mention that you know the plan and assume you are included. For example, if your two friends are going on a bike ride to the park, you might say, "I was about to go on my bike, so I can meet up with you guys." You are not really asking a question here, but more like assuming you are automatically welcome. Most of the time this will work out, but if they said "Actually we were just going to go ourselves," you could reply with, "Ok, cool. Have fun and I'll talk to you guys soon." One boy I know did this and then went on a bike ride with his other friend to their middle school parking lot. They ran into the two other kids and the four of them ended up hanging out. (Keep in mind that, overall, your good friends should care about your feelings and welcome you to join them.)

2. **SHOW CONFIDENCE.** Do what Carly did and don't make a big deal about it. Keep it casual, keep it cool, then talk about how it felt with someone like a parent so you don't have to feel this way alone.

3. **REGROUP AND ADAPT.** Tell them "that sounds good—have fun you guys. I'm going to catch up with my camp friend." Saying something like this is showing good coping and that you can adapt, and also letting them know that you're going to do something else, so you don't totally rely on them for your social life.

4. **SPEAK UP AND TALK!** Talk openly about it with your friends. It may have been an innocent mistake, but you should be able to go to your friends and talk about your feelings. If it turns out that it's more about social power (meaning that you were not included on purpose, rather than by mistake or randomly), then you might want to use a different strategy and talk to your friend openly about how you are upset. A good friend will care about your feelings and include you. If not, give your friend another chance. Look for patterns, and if you are consistently not included, then that brings up the idea that you may not be respected by your friends and may want to look into a different group.

Finally, if you have a bossy friend who always wants to do things their way, you need to decide how to challenge it. You can either go along with it and let them be the decision-maker, or you may decide that this is not working for you. If that's the case, you'll need to talk to your friend. Say something like, "I'd like us to take turns and sometimes do what I'd like to do." If there is push-back, then you could say something like, "So does it always have to be your way?" **BEING ASSERTIVE LIKE THIS IS APPROPRIATE WHEN YOU HAVE A BOSSY FRIEND, AND MUCH OF THE TIME, IT WILL IMPROVE THE RELATIONSHIP.**

Take-Away!

Social power struggles will come up from time to time with friends, even best friends. Be prepared and expect that it will happen. With a little advance planning, you can figure out how you will deal with it when it does happen. Remember that the goal is always equal power: mutual respect and mutual generosity. Try to not take things personally, and give your friends the benefit of the doubt. But if there is an issue, assert your rights in the friendship by joining in, showing confidence, regrouping and adapting, and/or speaking up and telling your friend how you feel.

Chapter 5

Rebalance Power Imbalances & Struggles

ow we're going to focus on social power struggles that come up with kids that are not your friends or are kids you don't even know. Remember that social power issues exist on a spectrum!

```
Mild ——————————————————————— Extreme
     Ignoring    Teasing      Threatening
     Excluding   Putting down  Name      Bullying
                 /criticizing  calling   Physically hurting
                                         Emotional Abuse
```

When facing any social power struggle, the skills to keep in mind are the same:

- believe in yourself (have self-confidence)
- stick up for yourself (be assertive)
- focus on what you can do, what actions you can take to change the situation (find your internal locus of control)

Many times, social power issues come up when you are trying to join a group. You have already read about not asking to join and some ideas of how to handle it when you make effort to join but they are not welcoming. Here's another idea: think of the **DOs** and **DON'Ts** of social power as rules to live by.

✓ DOs

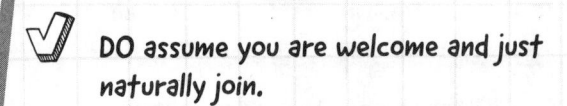

- ✓ DO assume you are welcome and just naturally join.

- ✓ DO be assertive and stick up for yourself.

- ✓ DO be direct and say, "Don't talk to me like that" (this is more of a command, and not an ask) or "Sorry, who do you think you are again, talking to me like that?" (this is showing that you don't just take put-downs from others).

- ✓ DO dismiss the other kid's attempts to have power over you by challenging it (for example, make a joke of it, be sarcastic, laugh it off to show you don't take it seriously).

- ✓ DO show confidence: express your preferences, opinions, put it out there (this shows you are not simply defaulting to what others want).

- ✓ DO be willing to find new kids to hang out with.

DON'Ts

- ✗ DON'T ask to join.

- ✗ DON'T ask others to be nice (or nicer) to you.

- ✗ DON'T tell others that what they did hurt your feelings (as this strengthens their power as it shows how much they can impact you).

- ✗ DON'T ask a parent (or another adult) to solve this social problem for you by talking to the other kid's parent (unless it's actual bullying).

- ✗ If someone is putting you down, DON'T ask them to stop. Also, don't be passive and just ignore them. Instead, use social power strategies.

Any time you **ASK**, you are **GIVING THE OTHER PERSON THE POWER** as they can either give you what you want or not; the control is in their hands. It's a bit confusing because you are taught to be nice and polite, and asking if you can be a part of the group seems to fit with that model.

THE KEY IS TO KEEP YOUR POWER AND NOT GIVE IT AWAY.

The same is unfortunately true if you ask someone to treat you better and tell them that your feelings are hurt; this affirms their power because now they see the effect they have on you. Now they see that they can make you upset. In close, safe friendships, of course you can be vulnerable and share that your feelings are hurt, but not with those who are trying to have power over you, or those that are mean and hurtful to you on purpose (since it will only make their power stronger). Remember: there are **DOs** and **DON'Ts** when it comes to social power.

When someone you don't know treats you badly, whether they are not nice, insulting to you, or making fun of you, this means that they have given themselves permission to overpower you. To stop this, you have to let them know that they **DON'T HAVE YOUR PERMISSION** to treat you this way. Remember in the beginning when we looked at the definition of social power and how for someone to have power, it needs to be **PERCEIVED** as legitimate? Well, if you don't see their power as real power, then they don't have it. This is really where your power lies: if you don't validate the other person's power, then they don't have any power over you!

DON'T RECOGNIZE SOMEONE'S POWER OVER YOU AS LEGIT.

Look at the fourth **DO**—dismiss the other kid's attempt by challenging it and making a joke of it. Be sarcastic, laugh it off.

When you give verbal or non-verbal cues (like rolling your eyes) that you don't take what they are saying seriously, you are taking the power back. This is just one way to **STAND UP** to someone trying to have power over you, and if doing something this bold doesn't feel natural, that's okay; you can be just as direct with a more serious tone.

The main thing is that you must challenge their attempts to have power over you so it doesn't work. It's the mindset of *I have to assert myself*, followed by an assertive response.

YOU WANT TO HAVE THE MINDSET OF BEING ASSERTIVE!

PRO TIP

Before you read much more, take a minute to think about bullies. As we discussed in Chapter 3, in this book you are learning more to handle situations where others are trying to have power over you, but not hurt you or truly bully you. It may feel like they are a bully and you can even call them that, but there is a difference. Bullying tends to be more severe: you may be at risk of getting physically hurt, and it's often the same person who regularly bullies you (it can even seem like they are out to get you). Cyberbullying is another type of bullying that unfortunately happens quite a bit. There are helpful websites to figure out how to address this, which are listed in the Extra Resources at the back of the book.

If any bullying (in person or cyber) is happening for you, you need to tell your parent or another adult. If you want to stand up to the bully (if it is safe to do so), there is a great video on YouTube called "How to Stop a Bully" which is worth watching (the link to this is also in the back of the book under Extra Resources). In it there is a role play between an actor (bully) and speaker (acting as the bully's target) that shows how you can respond by not taking the bully seriously:

> Bully: You're an idiot.
>
> Target: Oh you think I am an idiot?
>
> Bully: Yeah.
>
> Target: Yeah, sometimes I do stupid things, that's true.
>
> Bully: Yeah, you do, you always do stupid things.
>
> Target: I know, you're so smart, you're so lucky.
>
> Bully: Yes, I am.
>
> Target: You're awesome.
>
> Bully: Thank you, and you're not.
>
> Target: I know, we established that, so look. My happiness is not based on whether you think I'm cool or not. I'm gonna to be happy even if you hate my guts... And I'll always be nice to you.

Now, what if there is someone that you thought was nice or felt positively toward (for example, maybe one of the neighborhood kids or someone in your extracurricular activities) and they end up being not nice to you? Remember that this means that this person is not someone who meets *your* criteria for friendship. It doesn't matter what they want, you won't let someone like that be your friend. This is the mindset that will help make it clear who is a good candidate for a friend and who is not. A lot of kids tell me that they aren't sure—maybe this girl is nice or maybe she isn't, or sometimes she is and sometimes she isn't—and to help them be clear, I explain that we wouldn't want a friend to be only sometimes nice!

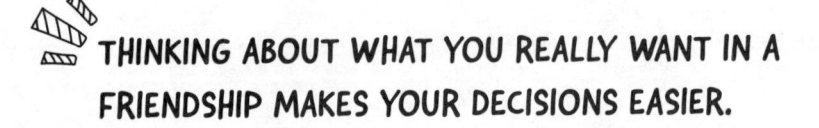

THINKING ABOUT WHAT YOU REALLY WANT IN A FRIENDSHIP MAKES YOUR DECISIONS EASIER.

Similarly, if others who were your friends suddenly turn on you and push you out of the group, at this point, they are moving from friend to non-friend and in addition to recognizing that you have to change to new friends (a challenging but common situation for many middle schoolers), you also have to assert yourself and deal with it as a social power issue. When you have the **EXPECTATION OF EQUAL POWER, MUTUAL RESPECT AND MUTUAL GENEROSITY, AND MAKE SURE TO HAVE FRIENDSHIPS THAT FIT THAT STANDARD,** you will find yourself with high quality, meaningful relationships!

Take-Away!

Dealing with social power struggles is something everyone must face. The goal is to stand up for yourself and not be passive. It's also important to remember: don't give your power away and don't recognize someone else's power over you as legitimate. The next chapter is going to have six detailed examples of kids who navigated social power issues very well. Learning from them as a model will help you feel more prepared to handle these struggles in your own life.

Chapter 6

Inspiring Stories

Many kids have dealt with social power issues that have really been challenging for them, taking up a lot of mental energy and focus. You might be dealing with similar struggles with friends and classmates yourself. It might be helpful (and interesting!) to read about how these six middle schoolers navigated social power struggles successfully.

Read closely and note how being assertive, showing confidence, developing personal agency, and overall staying true to oneself really can make a difference and balance out social power dilemmas. If you have to look back at previous chapters for tips on assertiveness, confidence-building, and what the heck personal agency is, it's OK to take a minute and review. Uncomfortable situations and social power dilemmas can be a struggle for sure. It takes some practice to be assertive, but you totally have what it takes to do this.

FOR EXAMPLE!

THE BACKSTORY: You might remember Maya, who was part of a three-person best friendship with Ashley and Taisha. Over the summer, they became friends with two other girls, Sasha and Lila. Maya experienced Sasha pushing her out of the group; first she made some subtle digs at Maya and was dismissive. Then she invited Ashley and Taisha over, without including Maya; they made a TikTok and posted pictures on Instagram. This was the first time Maya hadn't been included with Ashley and Taisha and she couldn't help but feel betrayed by them. Every time the five of them had lunch together, Maya was ignored by Sasha. Sasha talked over Maya and interrupted her, wanting all of the attention to stay on her. One time, after Maya said she was going away for the weekend with her family, Sasha said to the other girls, "The four of us should get together this weekend," which meant that Maya wouldn't be included. Maya came home and cried to her parents; she felt hurt and was stressed out. She was really upset that Ashely and Taisha didn't stand up for her and say something to Sasha to suggest that they all make a plan when Maya was available.

THE SOCIAL POWER FIX: Maya came up with a three-part strategy she could try to change this situation:

1. Maya would invite all four of them to her house and make a lot of effort to have fun with Sasha. Her house would be her turf and she'd naturally have more control over the situation.

2. Maya would make plans with Ashley and Taisha to re-connect with them, since she was feeling hurt and wanting to repair their friendship. When they were together, Maya would casually mention how she felt excluded a few times recently and also wonder aloud if Sasha maybe didn't like her. By mentioning this, Maya could see how her friends would react or what their perspective was.

3. The next time Sasha interrupted her, Maya would be assertive and say "I was in the middle of saying something! As I was saying...." And the next time Sasha put her down, Maya would be assertive and stick up for herself directly with a comment such as, "Sasha, we don't talk like that to each other" and then look at Ashley and Taisha to acknowledge who she meant by "we." (Maya role-played and practiced this several times with me.)

THE RESULT: Maya's invitation was a success and the four girls came over after school one day; the five of them made TikToks together and had a great time. Sasha was a bit removed at first but after a little while, she seemed friendly and Maya went out of her way to connect with her—she stood next to Sasha during the TikToks and put her arm around her at the end of one. When they left, she hugged Sasha first then the other three to say good-bye.

Maya also had separate plans with Ashley and Taisha and without even having to say anything to them, Taisha commented on her own that she felt Sasha was really nice but "a little bossy," and Ashley agreed. Maya added that she felt a little upset when she wasn't included in the after-school hangout, and both girls were very understanding. Maya felt validated by their reactions, and it was great for the three of them to be together like old times.

Finally, there were a few times when Maya stood up for herself and pushed back a bit with Sasha. She used humor and felt confident as she called Sasha out for interrupting her. Maya said what she planned out but also playfully said, "We'll get to you in a moment, so stay cool…" and Sasha actually smiled.

All three strategies played out well for Maya, and she found some positive qualities in Sasha that ended up making her a pretty good friend. Maya still didn't want to hang out with her one-on-one but was happy to be with her in the group.

Take a Minute!

Here's the thing about loyalty in friendships. Although friends are certainly allowed to pair off and have plans separate from the whole group, it's also reasonable to expect that your friends will show loyalty to you. In a situation where one person is intentionally including everybody except you, it's fair to want one of your friends to mention that you should be invited or even not be willing to participate without you. This is particularly true when it comes to bigger events like parties or concerts. The closer the friendship—for example, if you have a best friend—the more reasonable it is to expect loyalty from them by making sure you are included.

FOR EXAMPLE!

THE BACKSTORY: Remember how Jay was given such a hard time by two kids at soccer, Ollie and Logan? They called him a "loser" and kicked the ball at him, while putting down his performance no matter whether they won or lost. Jay was a little shy and on the quiet side, so being assertive and facing his teammates with confidence was a bit hard for him. Plus, he wasn't used to standing up for himself since, before this, he hadn't had any kids be mean to him or mistreat him in any way! He was actually a very good soccer player. Ollie and Logan's behavior was partly because they were super competitive kids and also because they wanted to have power over him. Jay was super stressed about this and talked about quitting soccer, but that was not the right solution. Jay had the right to play the sport he loved and had worked hard to get onto this team! He shouldn't empower Ollie and Logan and let their behavior have this much influence in his life and prevent him from being on *his* team. And at some point in his life, Jay was going to have to face social power and this was his chance to learn the skills.

THE SOCIAL POWER FIX: Jay needed to first change his thinking in order to feel like he could assert himself. He thought about his rights and how he was being put in a position where he if he stayed passive, the situation would not change. He also understood that he had to be able to do this to defend himself. As he processed what this was like for him, Jay started to get really mad (which was great, because anger can often motivate us to take action!). He role played what to say and how to say it. Jay practiced a range of come backs (some sarcastic) such as:

> Stay in your own lane. Enough with your stupid comments.

> Are you done yet? What else do you want to say about me?

> You guys are soooo cool, I'm soooo impressed with how cool and amazing you both are!

> You win the award for good sportsmanship. It's going to take you so far in life.

> If you keep going, you're probably going to get kicked off the team. Coaches don't put up with this.

He also planned for what they could say back and how he would handle it at that point. He did something called **STRESS INOCULATION** (something that you will learn in more detail in the next chapter), which allowed him to anticipate what they could say back to his comebacks and be prepared for how to handle that as well. After weeks of practicing, he felt confident (though also nervous) and was able to talk back to them.

Since they messed with him at most practices, he was prepared. Jay went to practice the same way as usual and then when Logan teased him again, he said a combination of the comments he had prepared. Most of all, he stood up straight, looked Logan right in the eye, and used a firm and reasonably loud voice. Then he walked away from them; he heard them whispering something to each other after that. The next practice, he played better than usual. Ollie said one more comment to him, which was a challenge to the social power Jay had shown: "Are you going to give us a hard time this week again?" and Jay replied with, "Sure am" and "Also, you should know that everyone is watching both of you." Everyone could see Jay's confidence!

THE RESULT: After standing up to them at the two practices, Ollie and Logan left him alone and Jay began to enjoy soccer again. They ignored him but Jay was fine with that; Jay also made a point to look at them here and there, and not look away. By doing this, he was showing assertiveness in his eye contact and body language and communicating that he wasn't afraid of them.

The best part of how well things turned out was the confidence that Jay felt, which came from his sense of taking charge of the situation by making a plan and executing it. This also helped him develop more personal agency (again, this is when you believe you can do a specific task and have the skills that are needed to do it). He realized that he could impact a situation that felt out of his control, which also strengthened his sense of an internal locus of control, giving him the confidence that he could do it again if he ever encountered a similar situation.

This is a perfect example of when social power issues need to be tackled. Jay had begun to dread going to soccer and his parents had even noticed. But Jay had the right to enjoy his sport and be free to play on his team without being harassed. When social power struggles create an interference in your life, as they did for Jay, it's even more important to handle them head-on.

FOR EXAMPLE!

THE BACK STORY: Ami loved gymnastics and she had been doing it for many years, literally since she was in pre-school! She had a group of friends from gymnastics and most of them were on her team, though most of them went to different schools. They spent a lot of time together—like six days a week—and she always felt comfortable. This year, a new girl, Gina, joined her team. Gina had also been doing gymnastics for years, but at a different gym. As soon as Gina arrived, Ami felt some tension from her; it seemed like Gina made a lot of effort with the other girls but not with Ami. On a few occasions, she talked over Ami, disagreeing with what she was saying. Also, when they were practicing for meets, Gina cheered several of the other girls on, but never said anything encouraging or positive to Ami.

As the weeks went by, Gina said more and more insensitive things. Ami's parents were divorced (which Gina knew) and when Ami's dad came to pick her up, Gina commented, "It must be the worst to have to go between two different homes. I'm so glad I don't have to do that." Another time, Gina had several of the girls (but not Ami) over to her house and later, in front of Ami, talked about how much fun they all had. Li, another teammate, had the whole team join her for her birthday dinner at a restaurant. Ami found out that Gina was texting the other girls about making a plan for after the dinner that did not include Ami. Ami's other teammate told her about it and stuck up for Ami by replying:

> If we do anything after this, all of us will be going.

THE SOCIAL POWER FIX: It was very helpful that Ami's teammate stuck up for her on the text, and it also made Ami realize that everything she was feeling was valid. She kept thinking about what she could have done wrong, if she said anything that wasn't nice, or if she wasn't welcoming enough to Gina when she joined the team; yet each time she tried to figure it out, it became clear that it was just that Gina wanted to have more power than Ami.

So the plan was for Ami to confront Gina directly. The next day, Ami told Gina that she wanted to talk with her for a few minutes after practice. She didn't *ask* to talk to Gina, she simply said, "After practice, we need to talk for a few minutes." Ami called Gina out directly and said, "Listen, you joined this team and I have been only nice to you. What you did at Li's dinner was totally uncool. These are my friends and my team and I will welcome you as long as you can be nice. That's on you." Ami also talked to her coach about the problem and the coach also had a conversation with Gina. Ami was close to her coach and she knew that her coach was good at solving social problems that sometimes came up in the group.

THE RESULT: After both Ami and the coach talked to Gina, she stopped the insensitive comments and made more of an effort to be nice to Ami. She apologized for what she did at Li's party and Ami handled it gracefully: she told Gina that she thought they should have a fresh start. Gina was relieved. Ami also made an effort to be kind and inclusive of Gina. They had no other issues after that.

FOR EXAMPLE!

THE BACKSTORY: Peter was in honors math class. Math was his favorite subject. One of his friends, Chris, was very competitive with him. Chris was always asking Peter how he did on the homework and tests. When they finished a test, Chris asked Peter how long it took for him to do it, and commented that he finished quickly and was one of the first to hand it in. Chris also put Peter down, even though he said it in a joking way, making comments about how Peter wasn't as good as him in math. Chris was also in honors science and Peter was in regular. Chris asked him if he thought he'd ever "make it into honors science." Peter found all of these comments super stressful and it made him on edge and also made him not want to talk to Chris, even though outside of these conversations, Chris was a good friend. In fact, Peter said that he likes Chris more than most people, so this conflict around competitiveness was really upsetting to him.

THE SOCIAL POWER FIX: Since Peter really valued his friendship with Chris, he decided to speak with him directly about it. The social power dynamic was a bit more subtle than in some other cases since Peter saw Chris as competitive, not necessarily as trying to have power over him. But, Peter understood that by Chris constantly comparing himself to Peter and pointing out the ways in which he was better than Peter, it was a social power problem.

Peter felt most comfortable texting Chris about this. That next week, Chris texted him about the quiz grades and asked what he got. Peter replied with:

Peter

> I'm sure you did great and I'm fine with my grade but when we talk about grades and how quickly we're getting our work done, it bothers me and makes me feel like we are in a competition. I don't want to be mean but it's annoying.

Chris

> I guess you got a bad grade then

Peter

> No, I didn't at all but it's not about what we got, it's about how it feels when you ask me about it. I think we should just not talk about math or grades for a bit.

Chris

> K.

Peter

> And you know you're one of my best friends so thanks.

THE RESULT: Peter's text was like magic. Chris responded well to it and the next time they spoke, he didn't mention anything about school or math. In math class a few days later, he made a comment to Peter about what they were learning, saying "this is so easy," then a minute later said "sorry, I didn't mean to say that." Peter made a joke and they laughed. Chris was able to change, and their friendship was better after that. Peter was even able to give compliments to Chris about things that had nothing to do with school. Because they had such a close friendship, being honest and direct was the best approach, and the social power dynamic was quickly corrected.

FOR EXAMPLE!

THE BACKSTORY: Eleanor had a group of friends that had more drama than she'd like; some of them were pretty judgy and they spent a lot of time talking about who was upset and about what. There were other girls who were friends with her friends that she knew but wasn't really friends with. One girl, Aliana, posted a TikTok about this expensive brand of sweatpants and how much they cost and said "like who would ever wear those to sleep?" This was targeting Eleanor, who wore this brand of sweatpants the day before in one of her own TikToks, which she made in the morning while hanging out in her room. Eleanor knew it was about her and that Aliana, who followed her on TikTok, made an assumption that she slept in the sweatpants. Those fancy sweatpants were actually a gift from her parents and were very special to her, and she felt offended at how Aliana made it seem like she just had them and didn't really care about them. She wanted to tell Aliana all that, but why should she feel like she owed Aliana an explanation, especially when Aliana was being so judgmental? If she explained herself in any way, she would be validating Aliana and not addressing the social power problem.

THE SOCIAL POWER FIX: Once Eleanor understood that this was about social power and how she would never say something like this about someone else, she was clear about how to deal with it. She messaged Aliana and said,

Eleanor
> I saw your post and I know it's about me. Totally rude.

Aliana
> It's not about you, I promise.

Eleanor
> It is, but that's ok you can't admit it.

A minute later, Aliana took the TikTok down—she deleted it!

Aliana
> You made me feel so bad that I took it down. Sorry.

Eleanor
> Thanks and I'm really happy you did

THE RESULT: Clearly Aliana knew she messed up and was easy about fixing it, which was great. Eleanor felt proud of herself for taking action and for how well it worked out. She also learned about social power and not giving her power away, or letting others make her feel like she needed to explain or defend herself. Eleanor learned more about healthy boundaries in relationships.

FOR EXAMPLE!

THE BACKSTORY. Some kids chose to bother Kevin and his friends for no reason. One of the kids was a few years older and lived in the same neighborhood as Kevin. Anytime Kevin saw this kid around, he would give Kevin a bad look and say nothing to him. Once when Kevin was with two friends playing at the field behind their school, this kid and his friends came over to them and laughed at them, made fun of Kevin's missed catch, and said "happy birthday" even though they didn't know them at all (and it was not anyone's birthday). They drove their bikes close to them, pretending to almost hit them but turning away at the last minute, and laughed at them when they got startled.

THE SOCIAL POWER FIX: Kevin's situation was a little closer on the spectrum to bullying, but because he didn't actually feel threatened, he treated it more like social power. Kevin and his friends handled the situation perfectly. At first, they ignored the other kids, but when they rode their bikes close to them, Kevin said "Wow you guys are so cool. You can leave now." The other kids imitated them *"You can leave now"* and made some mocking noises. Kevin's friend Tim gave them bad looks and Kevin said "No really, leave" and they continued to play without even looking the other kids' way. Eventually, the kids biked away.

THE RESULT: Even though Kevin was really mad and stressed about the situation, he was happy he talked back to the other kids and held their ground by continuing to play without leaving the field. These kids were simply trying to have power over Kevin and his friends, because they were younger. He planned that he would handle it the same way if it happened again. Kevin added that they knew one of the other kids' younger sister and planned to say, "I'll let your sister know what a jerk you are." Whether they would have the chance to say this or not, it gave Kevin the confidence that they had something to fight back with should they need it. It was a good outcome largely because Kevin felt prepared to defend their power.

Take-Away!

What do you think of how these kids handed their social power dilemmas? Has anything like this happened to you? These six kids all had to deal with social power situations that they wished they could've avoided, but all six managed to assert themselves, stay true to themselves, and show confidence and personal agency. As much as everyone would like to avoid uncomfortable situations such as these, by facing them directly and using a social power approach, you build confidence and resilience by learning that you can handle whatever comes your way.

Chapter 7

Practice Takes Practice

I love my job. I mean I *really* love my job. I get to hang out with kids and teens and help them with all kinds of problems. One of my most favorite things to do (which is not always met with the same degree of enthusiasm ☺) is role-play! When I say "okay let's role-play it" I usually get an impressive grunt or eye roll, but I don't let it stop me...because I KNOW the incredible **POWER OF BEING PREPARED,** which is important for so many things, but particularly valuable when it comes to dealing with social power problems.

In this chapter, the goal is to get you to role-play! You will need to come up with your own social power situation that you want to learn how to tackle (a real-life situation is best) and we'll come up with a plan and then design a role-play to master that plan.

PRO TIP

Believe it or not, your self-confidence increases from the moment you begin developing a plan, and it grows when you practice that plan. By role-playing and practicing exactly what you will say and how you will say it, you become confident in expressing yourself in these tough situations. Through the role-play practices, it starts to feel natural and automatic.

First things first. You need to design the role-play before you can actually practice it and then actually do it in real life. It's best if you plan and prepare instead of just winging it, trust me!

As you read through these next pages, it will be helpful to think of a situation in which someone tries to have power over you or gives you a hard time or always seems to put you down. It can be a friend, someone you don't know, or even a family member like an older cousin.

So, **STRESS INOCULATION** is when we prepare you to handle a situation in a very specific way. Basically, you:

- **PLAN FOR WHAT YOU WILL SAY,** then plan for the various things the other person could say back, and how you will respond to each of them.
- Pick three possible outcomes: **EASY, MEDIUM, AND HARD,** and decide how you will respond, how they will respond to you, and what you will say back.
- Plan for the back-and-forth dialogue in the three possible outcomes so you end up being very **PREPARED FOR WHATEVER COULD COME YOUR WAY.** The goal is for it to feel natural for you to respond to each of the possible outcomes, including when you need to be very assertive and really challenge the other person.

It's helpful to keep in mind that Easy, Medium, and Hard describes how quickly it takes for the person to meet your goal of them not trying to have power over you. It could be *really hard* for you to talk back and say assertive comments and stick up for yourself, but if you do it once or twice and the other person changes their behavior, then it would count as easy because it didn't take long to get them to change.

When you challenge someone's social power attempts over you, there are a variety of possible outcomes; it could go smoothly and be relatively easy, or it could be hard and really uncomfortable, or somewhere in-between. **Stress inoculation** helps you be prepared for the different ways it could go, and role-playing the scenarios makes it flow easily. Not only does making and practicing these detailed scenarios make you feel prepared, but this **PREPARATION BUILDS YOUR CONFIDENCE!** It makes you feel like you can do it AND it makes you come across as a natural. The best part is that for most situations, you will usually find that you didn't need most of the preparation you did, because the situation usually ends after one or two exchanges!

How to Prepare, AKA Stress Inoculation Plan

1. Come up with what you will say in response to someone's social power attempt.

2. Generate three different ways the person or other people could react to what you say:

    a. **EASY:** they respond well and change their behavior almost immediately;
    b. **MEDIUM:** they give you some push back, continue to challenge your social power for a bit longer before changing their behavior; or
    c. **HARD:** they give you a lot of push back and you have to keep going back and forth and may even need to involve others (including adults) before they change.

3. Plan out how each response could go, what they could say, then what you will say back, and map it out for three or four different back and forth sequences.

4. Role-play and practice it, record yourself and improve how you sound, how you look, how you stand, and so on. Engage others in your practice and keep doing it until you feel confident and saying these things feels easy and automatic.

To show how this is done, let's use one of the examples from the last chapter: Jay and the soccer teammates who tried to have power over him. Here's Jay's Easy, Medium, and Hard options:

✓ EASY

Jay stopped being passive, stuck up for himself, and Ollie and Logan immediately stopped giving him a hard time. He only had to do this for two back-and-forths and then the dynamic changed permanently. While it was hard for Jay to do this, and he had to get his thinking back on track first, the outcome was easy to get to: he made the effort and they responded well. Jay got them to stop bothering him in a pretty short period of time and by only having to say something twice. (If you remember the last chapter, this is exactly how it worked out for Jay!)

> Stay in your own lane. Enough with your stupid comments. Got anything else to say or are you done yet?

> Are you going to give us a hard time again this week?

> Sure am. Also you should know that everyone's watching you both.

Ollie and Logan left Jay alone after that. They ignored him and actually stayed in their own lane. Jay's soccer performance improved.

MEDIUM

In this scenario, Jay assumed Logan would tease him again at the next practice, even after Jay stood up for himself, and Jay would start out the same way. Jay would say the first two comments again, while standing up straight with a firm voice and maintaining eye contact.

> Stay in your own lane. Enough with your stupid comments. Got anything else to say or are you done yet?

This time, Jay imagined that Logan would challenge him and say something rude like,

> I've never heard you talk before. I have a lot I could say.

Then Jay role-played (again with a confident stance) challenging him back.

> Well don't. I'm done with hearing your voice.

He imagined Logan would give him a bad look and whisper to Ollie, but not say anything to Jay.

Jay would then say something like, "Good, you're learning."

HARD

In this most challenging scenario, Jay planned that he would make even more effort but not get a good result and would need to talk to the coach in order for a change to happen. Jay was really uncomfortable with the idea of doing this, but it would be his last resort and was worth practicing just in case. Besides, it strengthened his confidence and sense of agency to know it was an option and to practice it.

"Stay in your own lane. Enough with your stupid comments. Got anything else to say or are you done yet?"

In this scenario, he assumed that after Jay asked if they had anything else to say, Logan would quickly reply,

> Yes, a lot. You suck and I don't know why you're on this team. Such a loser.

Jay would need to come back strong and not lose his confidence from this. He imagined he'd say,

> I figured, since you can't seem to stop talking. You win the award for being the best sport. You'll probably get kicked off the team.

He expected Logan might sarcastically say something like,

> Oooh, I'm really scared.

and Jay would confidently reply with

> You should be. And it will be embarrassing for you.

then walk away.

At this point, Jay would need to call the coach and tell him what was going on and ask for support.

The coach was approachable, and Jay had a positive relationship with him; even though Jay was shy, the coach always tried to make him feel comfortable and valuable to the team. Jay imagined the coach would respond with empathy and would talk to Ollie and Logan about how their behavior is unacceptable and could get them kicked off the team. He also imagined the coach would email both sets of parents.

After that, he figured Logan and Ollie would keep to themselves, and Jay would keep his head up high and play better.

As mentioned, you usually don't need all the preparation that you get from coming up with three different possible scenarios, but doing this has benefits. When it all plays out, being so prepared makes it flow smoothly and makes you feel ready and, you guessed it: **CONFIDENT!**

Stress Inoculation Plan

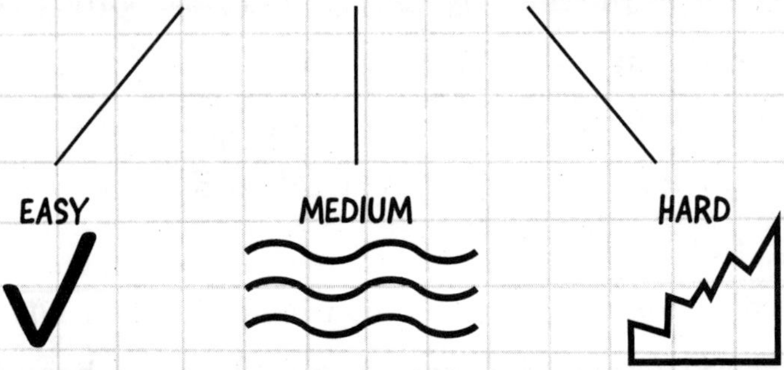

EASY ✓

MEDIUM 〰️

HARD 📈

What you will say,
what you think will happen,
and how you will respond in each situation.

What will happen
↘
How <u>you</u> will respond
↘
How <u>they</u> might respond
↘
What <u>you'll</u> say back
↙
Do this 4 times= fully prepared ✓

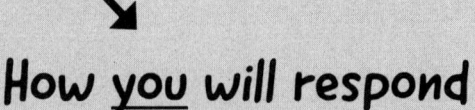

Grab a pen!

Now let's make your plan. It will help to write it out, so grab a piece of paper and a pen and start with these steps.

1. Identify the person who is giving you a hard time and trying to have power over you.
2. Describe the ways they try to have power over you: how they talk to you (tone of voice), what they say, and when they say it.
3. Consider what you can say in response that will challenge their social power and show them that you are no longer giving them permission to try to have power over you. Do this for three different scenarios: easy, medium, and hard.
4. Figure out what you need to do to improve your sense of confidence. What vibe are you giving off when you are around this person? Do you tend to look away or have trouble maintaining eye contact? Does your voice sound too low, or do you yell? Everybody has their own tendencies to look less confident when faced with someone they have a tense relationship with; the goal is to figure out what yours are and then practice doing the opposite.

Can you think about something that you became really good at by practicing?

TIME TO ROLE-PLAY!

Role-playing allows you to master the skills of challenging someone's social power attempts over you. By practicing it, you get better and better each time. When you practice with friends or family members, you're one step closer to actually doing it and being prepared when the situation arises. You will be able to say it all fluently and it will feel natural. You can master it with practice! Kids who role-play tend to do much better in the actual situations.

1. **DEVELOP YOUR STRESS INOCULATION PLAN.** Plan out exactly how someone (you) can respond to the person trying to challenge your power. Come up with a very detailed plan for what you will say in the Easy, Medium, and Hard scenarios. Many kids like to type it all out first.

2. **RECRUIT HELP AND A SUPPORT TEAM.** Ask family members or even a close friend to participate in your role-play. You could even ask a trusted adult—aunt or uncle, or a teacher or your school counselor—if you'd feel more comfortable with them.

3. **ROLE-PLAY!** Role-play the three situations—Easy, Medium, and Hard: start with you being the "aggressor," meaning that you will first model how the person who is trying to have social power over you sounds. Really try to get into the role and mimic how they sound, the words they use, how they stand, and so on. Then, repeat the role-plays with your family member or close friend becoming the aggressor, while you then practice being in your role and how you will respond.

4. **PRACTICE!** Do this over and over! If you can, it's helpful to make an audio or video recording of it so you can listen back or look back to see what you can do to improve it. You can adjust your body posture or tone of voice from seeing how you look or hearing how you sound. It can feel unnatural or you may even be embarrassed to record it, but even if you are the only one listening or watching back, it will be super helpful for you.

5. PRACTICE SOME MORE! Keep practicing until it becomes automatic for you, until you feel like you have really nailed down what to say and how to say it: keep practicing until you <u>own</u> it!!

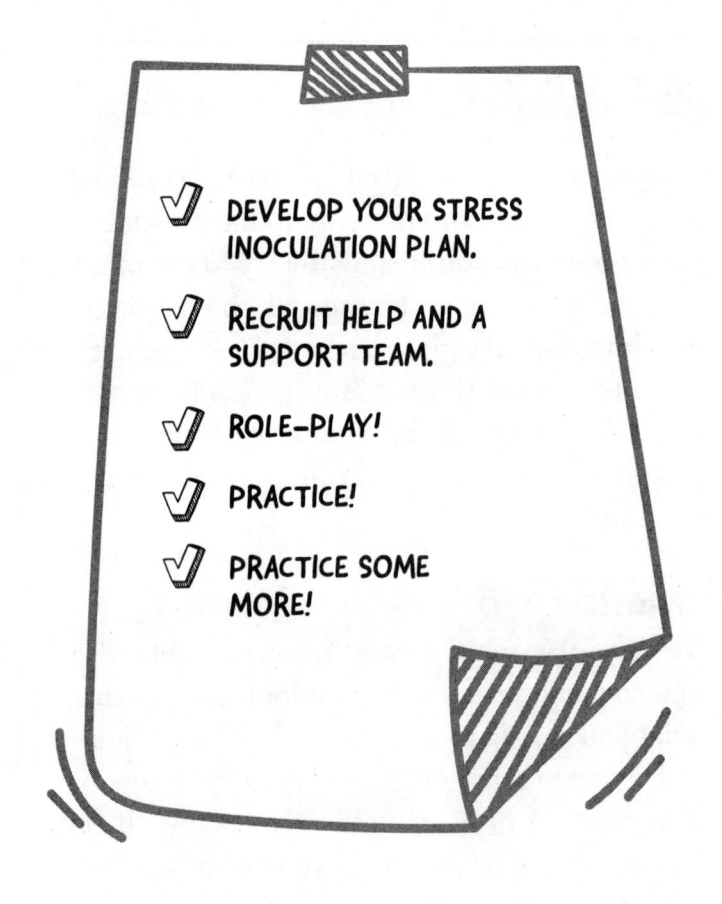

- ✅ DEVELOP YOUR STRESS INOCULATION PLAN.
- ✅ RECRUIT HELP AND A SUPPORT TEAM.
- ✅ ROLE-PLAY!
- ✅ PRACTICE!
- ✅ PRACTICE SOME MORE!

Take-Away!

This chapter should leave you feeling prepared and confident about handling a social power dilemma in your own life! A good Stress Inoculation plan means you plan for three scenarios: easy, medium, and hard. Then practice those scenarios with role-plays until you feel confident and prepared. Remember that role-plays make it all happen, and while it may feel a little silly to act it all out, it leaves you prepared; no one regrets doing role-plays!

Chapter 8

#SocialPower Dynamics

Technology is amazing and offers so much that makes your life better. Your parents have probably gone on and on about how different it was for them when they were growing up. Well, it was! If someone had something to say to you, they had to say it to your face. Now, you can text it, which often makes it easier to say, but sometimes *too* easy.

So sometimes people end up sounding less nice, less sensitive, and often are willing to say things that they would never be able to say to someone's face. This is the downside of technology, and as you know, a lot of unkind and judgmental things can be said over social media.

Social power issues can surface in texts, comments on Instagram, TikTok, and Snapchat... any form of social media! The other challenge that comes with texting and social media is the ease of writing things to influence others. This gives social power another stage, and online social power struggles can arise from friends and non-friends alike.

As said by many people, "With great power comes great responsibility." Think of social media in that way. Simply meaning that, if you do something, make sure that you do it for the good of others. If you can stop something unkind from happening, do it. **EASY RIGHT? LOL.**

Have you had something unpleasant said to or about you over text or social media?

Like all social power dilemmas, there is a wide range of virtual encounters. Perhaps social power dilemmas come up in a group chat or an Instagram comment or a TikTok video where you are not included (like what happened when Maya saw the TikTok of Sasha, Ashley, and Taisha). Not only did Maya experience **FOMO** (fear of missing out) but it was clear that Sasha did the video, in part, to establish social power over Maya. Not only did she feel badly for not being invited, but it was also only by seeing the TikTok video that she found out that there even was a plan and that she wasn't included!

FOMO can often come up when you see photos or videos that are posted without you, leaving you feeling like you are not as popular or as well-liked as your peers or friends. Sometimes, by not being included, it appears that someone else has more power than you. Sasha *appeared* to have more power than Maya when she posted the TikTok with Maya's two best friends—it *appeared* that the three girls were a group, even though *in reality*, Maya was closer to Ashley and Taisha and *in reality*, Ashley and Taisha had some negative feelings toward Sasha that were not visible in the video.

Have you ever felt upset or like you were missing out when you saw a picture or video of your friends doing something without you?

This idea of "appearance" is another thing to understand: a photo or even a video is just one brief moment in time. It doesn't tell the whole story, just a small part, and can be completely made up.

VIRTUAL IS NOT THE SAME AS REALITY.

Even virtual friendships, which may be very meaningful, are not often the same as real-life friendships. Remembering the difference between what you see on the screen and what really *is real* is important because it protects you from not reacting to things that may not be accurate.

Other times, the social power struggle is more direct, where someone is sending you mean texts, calling you names, confronting you over text, or spreading rumors about you. It could be a group text, where a few friends are calling you out on something you're doing or for something they don't like about you. This is especially hard, since when it's more than one person, you are automatically at a disadvantage. It could also be that someone is texting from someone else's phone and pranking you or pretending that they are someone else; this can be a **SOCIAL POWER DILEMMA.** Finally, it could be outright bullying where someone is threatening you or saying terrible things about you or sending you inappropriate pictures or making inappropriate requests over social media or text.

Have you found yourself saying things you would never say in person but are willing to text or post online?

Again, when there are threats and it's a bullying issue or it's inappropriate or of a sexual or violent nature, it's time to involve a trusted adult. In these cases, not responding at all to the texts may be the best response. This is not being passive; since it's happening virtually, by not responding you are choosing to not give any power to whoever is threating or bullying you (this is different from walking away when it's in person, which is a passive response). When you don't reply at all, they don't even know if you saw the text or post. Plus, when it's actually bullying, we care more about safety than being assertive anyway.

The Studies Show...

- "Digital stress" comes from negative exchanges over text, social media, and chats. There are 2 types of digital stress:
  1. when mean or hostile messages to or about you are made virtually.
  2. stress involved with managing the closeness of your relationships virtually (like feeling pressure to go along with others' requests or feeling smothered by too many texts).

- Another study showed that almost 60% of US teens have experienced being bullied or harassed online:
  - the most common type is name-calling
  - 32% of teens reported that someone spread false rumors
  - 21% reported that someone (other than a parent) is always asking what they're doing or where they are or who they're with.

- A Royal Society for Public Health survey found that 14-24 year olds in the UK reported that social media took a toll on their mental health and overall wellbeing:
  - Instagram, Snapchat, Facebook, and Twitter led to increased anxiety, feeling depressed, and poor body image.

Before we go into some more examples and learn tips on how to best handle social power issues that come up virtually, let me remind you that the same social power skills apply:

- use **ASSERTIVENESS** by sticking up for yourself,
- be **SELF-CONFIDENT,** and
- remember your **PERSONAL AGENCY.**

We are just adapting these skills to the virtual world!

RELY ON YOUR ASSERTIVENESS SKILLS AND SELF-CONFIDENCE WHEN THE ISSUES COME UP IN VIRTUAL SITUATIONS.

Remember Eleanor, who had to deal with a friend of her friend group who made fun of her for having and (presumably) sleeping in her expensive sweatpants? If Eleanor had not seen Aliana's TikTok, she would never have known that she was being made fun of and would not have felt stressed, upset, and embarrassed. In this case, Eleanor dealt with it head on with confidence, and Aliana ended up taking the TikTok down. Because they had a friendly relationship, and because Aliana was actually a caring person who acted out of character by making such a TikTok, the situation resolved fairly easily.

FOR EXAMPLE!

Hayden was upset that Elijah, who was in his same group of friends, only posted pictures that Hayden wasn't in and never liked or commented on any of Hayden's posts even though he liked all of their other friends' posts and was very active on Instagram. Yet, Hayden liked all of Elijah's posts and often made positive comments. Since Elijah never liked or commented on Hayden's posts, there was definitely a subtle power dynamic. To fix this imbalance, Hayden decided to no longer make comments or even like Elijah's posts. Hayden also wouldn't post pictures of Elijah on his page, therefore mirroring what he was doing. Hayden didn't want to be mean, but Elijah was not showing him the same respect, so Hayden was making it more equal. After thinking more about this situation and the lack of mutual respect, Hayden realized that this was not a friendship he wanted to pursue.

Have you ever found yourself in a situation where your friends called you out over text?

FOR EXAMPLE!

Kerry had a group chat with four of her friends. Lead by one girl, they all complained that she was "being selfish" lately and "only talking about herself." As with a lot of these situations, it usually starts with one person saying something and the others either agreeing or not saying anything to defend the targeted person. Kerry felt so bad about this situation and ended up feeling like her friends were not her friends anymore and started thinking about other friend groups she could join. Kerry had to take a minute to realize she was catastrophizing and needed to step back and realize what was happening was plain old social power struggles. Not her at all! Kerry navigated the situation very well, ended the conversation over text and said that they can talk more about this in person, if it's that important, but she's not doing this over text.

Sometimes it's confusing to know if it is about a social power issue OR just a friendship issue.

#SocialPower Dynamics • 181

Sometimes you have to own up to something you've actually done wrong! In this case though, the leader was actually very judgmental and often trying to get others to agree with her and submit to her opinions. So Kerry decided to treat this as a social power issue with the lead girl and ignore the part about her friends joining in. It was clear that the issue was the lead girl trying to get power over her and not her friends actually having a real problem with her or her behavior.

If you were really feeling that your friend was acting selfish or too self-focused lately, how would you handle it?

Think about it: Would you call someone out over a group text with several other friends, or would you gently bring it up the next time you were with your friend in a one-on-one? Would you come across as aggressive or as kind? When it's done over group text, that's a big clue that it's a social power move, and you should treat it as such.

FOR EXAMPLE!

Michael was playing Fortnite with two of his friends and the others both started teasing him for not playing well and were mean about it. He was defending himself, but when this kept happening each time they played, he started to question if he should even be playing with them. At first, he was apologizing and stuck up for himself a bit by saying things like "come on, guys, this isn't cool" but eventually he had to say (offline, while not in a game), "I'm not going to keep playing with you guys if you treat me like crap. I have my other group to play with and I'll just play with them." At that point, they stopped completely. He set a boundary and it was respected.

If you receive random texts from peers who you are not friends with and aren't even in your contacts that are pranking, insulting, or being mean, you need to know how to best respond. Sometimes you will simply ignore it and just delete it. Other times, you might tackle it more directly. You could just respond and text Who is this?   if you don't know the number. And if the person still doesn't say who they are or keeps pranking you, you could text something like

> Great. I couldn't care less who you are, time to find a new hobby

and block the number. A move like that makes it very clear that you're not going to involve yourself with someone like that.

GOALS FOR VIRTUAL SITUATIONS AND SOCIAL MEDIA

In general, here are some guidelines to try when it comes to social media and anything virtual or online.

1. **STRIVE FOR MUTUAL RESPECT AND MUTUAL GENEROSITY.** These qualities are essential to a good friends and apply equally to all virtual situations as well as real life: texts, emails, social media, and when playing video games online.

2. **BE ASSERTIVE AND STICK UP FOR YOURSELF.** Don't be shy and let others put you down without talking back to them. Comments ranging from lightest to heaviest: "Not cool," "RUDE!" "Seriously?!" "Come on guys—enough," "I'm about to exit this chat," "I'm getting off now," "I'm not joking!" and "Are you having a bad day? You're acting like a jerk right now."

3. **STOP ENGAGING OVER TEXT.** Refuse to be involved in a group conversation over text where you are being targeted. Instead, suggest that you and one of the others in the chat get on the phone or, even better, over Facetime or in person, and talk about it in that context.

4. **START YOUR OWN CHAT.** For group texts/chats that you are not included in, don't try to get included—this gives your power away. Start your own chat and leave off whoever started the other chat and didn't include you. If they say anything, you can kindly and casually offer to start a new chat that includes everyone.

5. **BE THOUGHTFUL ABOUT WHAT YOU SAY AND POST.** Even on Snapchat (since someone can always take a screenshot), don't badmouth others. Try to be respectful and appropriate across the board.

> Ask yourself: would I be totally comfortable if my parent read anything I wrote? If not, don't text it!

6. BLOCK OR UNFOLLOW OR UNFRIEND BULLIES. Anyone who is doing any form of cyberbullying, or making inappropriate comments on your social media—block them and unfollow them. It's best to keep all accounts private so you can monitor who is able to see or comment on your posts.

7. STICK UP FOR FRIENDS. If you see someone trying to have social power over a friend of yours, on a group chat for example, you might consider sticking up for them. You could say "not cool" or "why are you acting like this?" or screenshot the conversation and text it to the person being mean with "I won't allow this on our chat so stop" or "I'll end this chat if you don't stop." Having that kind of leadership is amazing and a real sign of confidence; it's living your power in the world.

8. ASK FOR THE POST TO BE TAKEN DOWN. If someone posts something to embarrass you, like an unflattering photo of you, and it's clear it's a social power move, you can tell them to take it down. If they refuse, you could make a post such as a quote or random photo (not of the other person) that says something about others having to put people down to like themselves more and tag them in the post. It may sound like revenge, but when it's really just about the game of social power, and if they felt free to embarrass you, you need to come back with something that shows it didn't work.

Take-Away!

Just like social power struggles that happen in person, the goal is to know your rights and protect your power. You have the right to not be called names, be talked about behind your back, or have others be mean and disrespectful to you. Remember that you wouldn't treat others this way, so don't tolerate it when others give themselves permission to treat you badly. Again, being passive and not doing anything will not make the situation better—you must take action and be assertive and challenge the imbalanced power dynamic. You can do it!

Chapter 9

Do Some Healthy Thinking & Self-Talk

The way you think affects everything in your life. Your thoughts are your power. Positive messages will give you a boost and help you be better at solving social power problems. If you say negative messages to yourself about yourself, you will feel defeated and deflated even before you've taken any action. Be your own best supporter, talk to yourself as you would a best friend, cheer yourself on, and have self-compassion. Positive, compassionate, encouraging self-talk statements are just the support you need when you are navigating these issues.

THE VOICE IN YOUR HEAD SHOULD BE POSITIVE, ENCOURAGING, AND COMPASSIONATE!

Self-talk statements can definitely boost your confidence, particularly when you make changes to the way you think. By saying things like, "What would someone with strong self-confidence think in this situation? What would they do?" you put your mindset in position to have the best thoughts.

🖍 CHANGE THE WAY YOU THINK TO CHANGE THE WAY YOU FEEL.

Studies have proven the **POWER OF POSITIVE THINKING:** when people think positively, they grow more **neurons** in the left **prefrontal cortex** region of the brain. This part of the brain helps us handle problems, comes up with other solutions to solve them, and helps us stay balanced and have the right attitude. People who think negatively, on the other hand, grow more neurons in the right prefrontal cortex area of the brain, which is where uncertainty, negative moods, and pessimism come from. The more positive thoughts you have, the more neurons you will grow in the part of the brain that will lead to more positive thoughts. Also, when you are better able to solve problems, you will feel better and have more positive thoughts from that alone!

The same is true for negative thoughts: **THE MORE YOU HAVE THEM, THE MORE LIKELY YOU WILL GENERATE MORE OF THEM.** This highlights how important it is to produce positive thoughts; even if it feels fake at first, saying positive statements and will make it easier for you to feel real positive feelings. Try it! I know many kids who act positive in a kind of over-the top way and then report that it was either funny or the overly positive things they said actually worked.

Grab a pen!

Here's an activity to try. Get some note cards or small pieces of some paper (cut into little cards). Write down 10 or so positive statements. You can use ones from the list below or come up with your own. If you tend to be negative about certain things or certain situations, make some note cards that challenge your usual outlook at those times. Focus on the power you have to change your thoughts and look at a situation from a different angle.

- ☐ I've got this! I can do it!
- ☐ Things will work out for me.
- ☐ There is a lot I can do to make this better.
- ☐ What is within my control here? What efforts can I focus on?
- ☐ I believe in myself and am thinking of my past successes!
- ☐ What would someone who is self-confident think in this situation? What would they do?
- ☐ I can change the way I think to change the way I feel.

- ☐ I can be a positive force in my own life.
- ☐ Every problem has a solution.
- ☐ I know what I have to offer in a friendship and know its value.
- ☐ I can be assertive and stick up for myself.
- ☐ I've never regretted sticking up for myself.
- ☐ I have to act based on my values, not my feelings.
- ☐ What is the self-compassionate thing to say to myself?
- ☐ It's my right to be treated appropriately and expect others to be respectful.
- ☐ I will not give my power away!

Next, read these cards until you've memorized your favorite ones. The goal of this is to automatically think these things and change your mindset around when things are rough. It takes practice, but just like the cognitive-behavioral motto says: **YOU CAN CHANGE THE WAY YOU THINK TO CHANGE THE WAY YOU FEEL.**

Let's go back to Jay and how he had to change this thinking to see that what was happening with Logan and Ollie was social power and he had to be assertive. Once Jay was able to make this mental shift, he thought through different skills involved with challenging this situation and was encouraged to be positive about it. Jay decided to focus on **ACTUAL THINGS HE COULD DO THAT WERE WITHIN HIS CONTROL.** He cut himself some slack (had self-compassion) when he was worried about not being able to talk back to them. So Jay focused on supporting himself with positive, compassionate, encouraging self-talk and being positive that he was taking action.

When you are dealing with a social power issue or have friends who are mistreating you, it can feel like a lot of work. This makes it even more important to be positive, self-compassionate, and encouraging with yourself. Use these statements to support yourself when you are dealing with social power issues.

BE POSITIVE AND ENCOURAGING AND UNDERSTANDING WITH YOURSELF.

In addition to the benefits of positive thinking, there are also studies showing that positive friendships improve your sense of well-being. Healthy relationships are good for your health! Unhealthy relationships are bad for your health and negatively affect your energy. You can tell the difference: when you are around certain people, your energy is high and happy and you are better able to come up with creative ideas. The energetic space around you is light and supportive. When you are around others who are negative, critical, judgmental, or insensitive, it brings you down, closes you off, and limits your creativity. In Chapter 2, we discussed your rights in friendships from a social power perspective. Now let's take it to the next level and figure out which friendships are the healthiest and most positive.

HEALTHY, HAPPY FRIENDSHIPS IMPROVE YOUR SENSE OF WELL-BEING AND ARE GOOD FOR YOU!

People who support you, are considerate, respect your boundaries, and don't put down your ideas or opinions are excellent candidates for good, healthy friendships. They also celebrate the good things that happen to you, give you good energy, and encourage you to be your best you. Also, being a supportive, positive influence in your friendships will help you experience more positivity in your life as well. Anytime you can be a positive force for others, do so! Radiating with positive energy also builds your level of social competence, and over time, others will notice that they feel better when around you and your can-do attitude!

FOR MORE ABOUT THE RIGHT KIND OF PEOPLE, READ *VIBRATE HIGHER DAILY*. HIGHLY RECOMMENDED! CHECK OUT THIS AND MORE RESOURCES AT THE END OF THE BOOK.

Another amazing way to add in more positive energy to your life is to have a gratitude mindset, which is when you focus on what is going well and all of the many things you have in your life, whether it's good health, special relationships and connections, things you love doing, or any resources you are lucky enough to have. The practices of gratitude involve being attuned to and **MINDFUL OF ALL THAT YOU CAN BE GRATEFUL FOR** and putting your focus on that. People who are grateful have a better experience in life and less likely to have depression. If you always focus on the negative, you'll develop a deprivation mindset which is when you focus on what you don't have or what's not working out in your life. Again, it all comes back to where you put your energies and what thoughts you choose to have.

POSITIVE Thinking

INSTEAD OF... → SWITCH TO...

INSTEAD OF...	SWITCH TO...
It doesn't matter what I do, this kid is always going to give me a hard time.	I can use assertiveness skills and stick up for myself. I have more power than I realize, I just need to use it.
I can't stand going to soccer anymore. Maybe I should find a new team.	This is MY soccer team—I can't give these jerks so much power. I'm going to make it clear that I won't take this anymore!
I'm looking at all these posts—everybody is having so much more fun than me.	Social media is not reality and these social comparisons only make me feel bad. I'm taking a break from my phone and going outside.
My friend was so annoying—he was putting me down all day.	Sometimes a friend is having an off day. If it happens again, I'll deal with it and say something. Mutual respect is expected!
I hope those kids will let me play with them.	I'm going to naturally join their game and go in with a fun, positive attitude. If they are not nice, I wouldn't want to play with them anyway.
My older cousins are always talking down to me. I really don't want to go to the family BBQ.	This is my family BBQ and I have the right to be there and to be treated with respect. I'm going and when they give me a hard time, I will stick up for myself.

Take-Away!

When dealing with social power struggles, especially those that are ongoing, it can be easy to have negative thoughts and a deprivation mindset. In some ways, when you are in this mindset you're surrounded with negativity, and this gives more power to the social power dilemma and the person who is trying to have power over you. Rather than giving away your power, focus on gaining more power by learning ways to encourage a positive, gratitude mindset. As you approach these social power struggles with your new skills, you will have a different outcome, and this alone will make you feel better. But also remember that you are in control of what you focus on, and you are in charge of your feelings and actions.

Chapter 10

Strong & Resilient = Bright Future

Have you heard of the word **resilience**? Resilience is the ability to bounce back after setbacks and not let things stand in the way of your goals. Believe it or not, by working through social power dilemmas in your life and discovering your own power, you end up not only being more confident, but more resilient as well. Resilience is something that you can develop.

Whenever you are able to overcome an obstacle, or work through a problem by facing it head-on, you become better able to handle what comes your way down the road. Resilience allows you to cope better with social power struggles and stress in general. The magic about being resilient is that it is protective for you, because people who are resilient have better mental health (and are less likely to have anxiety and depression). Resilience is also associated with living longer and having greater satisfaction in life.

When it comes to developing resilience, one of the main things to do is to tackle problems when they arise, rather than trying to avoid dealing with them. Taking an active role in figuring out the problem and coming up with a plan to address it builds resilience. By addressing social power imbalances and planning how to respond to them, role-playing what you will say and how you will say it, and then actually doing the work involved (being assertive, talking back, sticking up for yourself, setting boundaries, and so on), you become more resilient. It's building your skill set so you will thrive as an adult!

TAKING AN ACTIVE ROLE IN FIGURING OUT THE PROBLEM AND COMING UP WITH A PLAN TO ADDRESS IT BUILDS RESILIENCE.

Healthy relationships and friendships and being resilient go hand-in-hand. Supportive relationships with peers, family members, and others in your life help you feel a **STRONGER FOUNDATION,** which builds resilience. As you think about this, remember that it's up to you to make sure that your friendships are the right ones, where your rights are being respected and where you have mutual respect and mutual generosity. So that's a good thing—you have the power to become resilient!

When you have a resilient mindset, you focus on managing obstacles and not letting anything stand in the way of your goals. Maya had to take action around dealing with Sasha, using strategies to balance out the power and re-establish the connection with her best friends. Jay had to manage the obstacle of Logan and Ollie's teasing to get back to enjoying soccer. Ami had to challenge Gina, using the solid relationship with her teammates as support as she did so. Peter had to be direct with Chris to enjoy his friendships with him again, and not feel pressure in math. Eleanor had to set a boundary with Aliana and be super assertive and clear with her. Finally, Kevin had to learn how to stand up to the mean kid in his neighborhood.

All of them had to step outside of their comfort zone and do things to change these power dynamics. They all had to prepare how they'd handle it, practice it over and over until it became automatic, and then use assertiveness to confidently deal with the social power struggle. It wasn't easy or comfortable, but it was worth it, as all of them were able to successfully change the situations. More importantly, all of them developed more self-confidence and more resilience. You should expect bumps in the road as you journey through your teenage years—it's not supposed to be

The Studies Show...

- One study found that mindfulness helps decrease stress and increase resilience. Self-compassion was an important part of the study's mindfulness program.

- Resilience is a protective factor when it comes to developing a mental health problem such as anxiety or depression. This means that resilient people are more likely to have better mental health.

- One study showed that resilient teens have higher self-esteem and have more problem-solving coping skills.

- These are 5 factors that lead to more resilience:
  - self-awareness
  - mindfulness
  - self-care
  - relationships
  - purpose

all smooth and perfect. If it was, you wouldn't develop the skills you need to handle being an adult! The goal is *not* to never have bumps; the goal is to manage them well and work through them with confidence and personal agency. In fact, the skills you learned in this book will not only help you when it comes to social power, but they will help you in a more general way as you grow up, make important decisions, and focus on being the best you in your life.

As you have more practice managing those times when someone tries to have power over you, it will get easier and easier and feel more natural to you. Also, others will see that they cannot have power over you and will stop trying. The confidence you project to others will give off the vibe that **YOU ARE TO BE TREATED APPROPRIATELY AND WITH RESPECT.** And, for those who don't get this message automatically, they will get it from you when you continue to stand up for yourself and respond with assertiveness.

Let's take a moment to reflect on everything you've read...

What I've Learned

SOCIAL POWER

Power = Equal

Power = Unequal

STICK UP FOR YOURSELF!

PERSONAL POWER

KNOW YOUR RIGHTS IN FRIENDSHIPS

POSITIVE THINKING, POSITIVE SELF-TALK, SELF-COMPASSION

PRACTICE & DO ROLE-PLAYS

BE RESILIENT

♡♡ SELF-CONFIDENCE ♡♡

SOCIAL COMPETENCE

MUTUAL RESPECT & MUTUAL GENEROSITY

SAFETY COMES FIRST!

INTERNAL LOCUS OF CONTROL

BE ASSERTIVE & STICK UP FOR YOURSELF!

SOCIAL POWER ONLINE

So are you about ready to take your power back? Remember to:

1. **FIND FRIENDS WHO RESPECT YOU.** Mutual respect and mutual generosity are the foundation for good friendships. Without it, social power becomes unequal and that can lead to power struggles and dilemmas.

2. **BE ASSERTIVE.** If you ignore social power dilemmas, nothing will change. Don't worry about coming off as mean. You must be assertive (not passive or aggressive) and stick up for yourself.

3. **BELIEVE IN YOURSELF.** Self-confidence is when you believe in yourself. You want to come across to others as self-confident, and this starts with *thinking and acting* like a person who has self-confidence. Sometimes you have to fake it 'til you make it, but eventually it will be true!

4. **SHOW PERSONAL AGENCY.** This is when you believe in your ability to do something and have the skills to do it. This will help you be motivated to get things done… and when you get things done, it grows even more personal agency!

5. **HAVE SOCIAL COMPETENCE.** Many social power dilemmas can be avoided all together by knowing how to join groups, connect with others, have empathy, and take another's perspective. In other words, being totally socially competent.

6. **ROLL WITH IT!** Know how to handle the situation when close friends challenge your power. Roll with it at first, then confront it or talk about it directly with them if it continues.

7. **LEARN FROM OTHERS.** Be inspired by the stories of kids who successfully dealt with social power struggles in their lives.

8. **PLAN OUT & ROLE-PLAY.** One big takeaway from this book is to remember the power of role-plays. Hardly anyone gets it right the first time! Plan out your role-play (stress inoculation) including what you will say and how you will say it. Practice it over and over until it feels natural for you.

9. **UNDERSTAND YOUR VIRTUAL WORLD.** Learn how to deal with virtual and online social power issues. Your friends are basically virtually connected 24/7, so there will likely be issues that come up over text and social media. Social media doesn't reflect reality. Only real life does!

10. **PRACTICE SELF-CARE.** Be nice and supportive of you! Compassionate, encouraging, and supportive self-talk and healthy thinking are crucial to your wellbeing and to the quality of your friendships. You can change the way you think to change the way you feel.

11. **DEVELOP A GRATITUDE MINDSET.** Focus on what is going well and what you have, not on what you don't have.

12. **WORK TOWARD RESILIENCY.** It's hard to stand tough in the face of adversity and stress. And this is next level-stuff—it takes patience and practice. But knowing that you can, and remembering how you've successfully managed obstacles and social power struggles before, will make each subsequent challenge easier and easier to deal with.

Congratulations on reading this book and learning all about social power. Good luck in the rest of middle school and beyond ☺

Acknowledgments

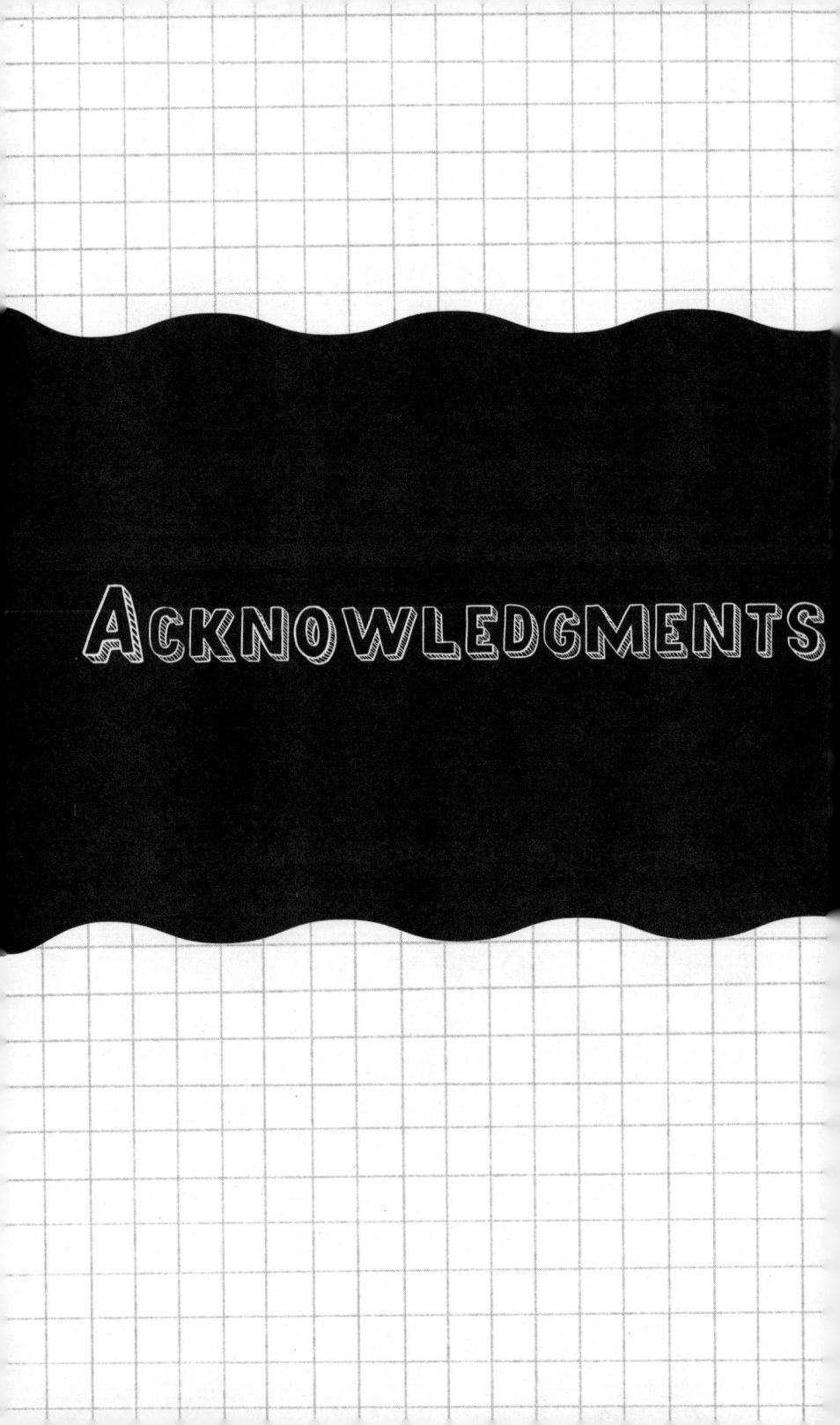

This book series would not have been possible if it wasn't for **Kristine Enderle's** vision, creativity, and commitment to providing the highest quality resources for children and teens. Thank you for choosing me as series editor and for all of your enthusiasm! Thank you to **Katie ten Hagen, Julie Spalding,** and **Rachel Ross** for their excellence and dedication to this series.

I couldn't be more grateful or prouder of **Dr. Silvi Guerra, Dr. Lenka Glassman, Dr. Anna Pozzatti,** and **Bonnie Massimino**. Without this team of outstanding authors, all devoted to excellence in helping children thrive, this series would not have come to be. I have loved every minute of our collaboration (even as it was all on Zoom)!

I am so grateful for my son, **Isaac:** you are my dream come true and somehow old enough to be in middle school! Thank you for being my "test subject" when writing this book and giving incredibly helpful ideas and feedback. Thank you for your continuous support in all I do, and for being so loving. You are in a league of your own, with your golden heart and kind soul. I love you beyond words.

I am so grateful for my younger son, **Todd:** you are my dream come true and while you've got a few more years to go before middle school, I know you will rock it! Thank you for your incredible enthusiasm about my writing and my work, and for being proud of me and always so loving. You are my heart and I love you more than you could ever know.

Thank you to my husband, **Brian:** Your ongoing support for my work is a true gift. Thank you for partnering with me on all the lessons and handouts we've done with our boys. I am so grateful for the extraordinary father you are and I love you with all my heart.

Thank you to my mentors, the ones who lie at the foundation of my success as a psychologist: **Dr. Rudy Bauer, Dr. Mary Alvord, Dr. Bernie Vittone, Dr. John McPherrin,** and **Dr. Harvey Parker.**

Finally, my *mother* would have loved this book; it's right up her alley. Among her many lessons, she taught me how to believe in myself, stick up for myself, and have self-compassion. She was the first to teach me the value of meaningful, authentic relationships, and was one who cherished her friends.

Extra Resources

Below is a list of other books and online resources that can further help you and your parents. Take a look to see which ones stand out to you, or might best support you to help with topics that can be challenging.

RECOMMENDED NON-FICTION BOOKS FOR TWEENS AND TEENS

Alvord, M. K., & McGrath, A. (2017). *Conquer negative thinking for teens: A workbook to break the nine thought habits that are holding you back*. New Harbinger Publications.

Carnegie, D. (1998). *How to win friends and influence people*. Pocket Books.

Covey, S. (2014). *The 7 habits of highly effective teens*. Touchstone.

Delia, L. (2019). *Vibrate higher daily: Live your power*. HarperOne.

Kay, K., & Shipman, C. (2018). *The confidence code for girls: Taking risks, messing up, & becoming your amazingly imperfect, totally powerful self*. HarperCollins.

Krimer, K. (2020). *The essential self-compassion workbook for teens: Overcome your inner critic and fully embrace yourself*. Rockridge.

Moss, W. L. (2021). *The friendship book*. Magination Press.

Sperling, J. (2021). *Find your fierce: How to put social anxiety in its place*. Magination Press.

Tompkins, M. T., & Martinez, K. (2010). *My anxious mind: A teen's guide to managing anxiety and panic*. Magination Press.

Zucker, B. (2022). *A perfectionist's guide to not being perfect*. Magination Press.

RECOMMENDED FICTION BOOKS FOR TWEENS AND TEENS

Craft, J. (2019). *New kid*. Quill Tree Books.

Patterson, J., & Tebbetts, C. (2012). *Middle school, the worst years of my life (Middle School, 1)*. Little, Brown and Company.

Reynolds, J. (2021). *Stuntboy, in the meantime*. Atheneum/Caitlyn Dlouhy Books.

Telgemeier, R. (2017). *Guts: A graphic novel*. Graphix.

Telgemeier, R. (2020). *Smile: A graphic novel*. Graphix.

RECOMMENDED BOOKS FOR PARENTS AND ADULT CAREGIVERS

Alvord, M. K., Grados, J. J., & Zucker, B. (2011). *Resilience builder program for children and adolescents: Enhancing social competence and self-regulation: A cognitive-behavioral approach*. Research Press.

Icard, M. (2021). *Fourteen talks by age fourteen: The essential conversations you need to have with your kids before they start high school*. Harmony.

Koplewicz, H. S. (2021). *The scaffold effect: Raising resilient, self-reliant, and secure kids in an age of anxiety*. Harmony.

Morin, A. (2018). *13 things mentally strong parents don't do: Raising self-assured children and training their brains for a life of happiness, meaning, and success*. William Morrow Paperbacks.

Stixrud, W., & Johnson, N. (2019). *The self-driven child: The science and sense of giving your kids more control over their lives*. Penguin Books.

Stixrud, W., & Johnson, N. (2021). *What do you say? How to talk with kids to build motivation, stress tolerance, and a happy home*. Viking.

Thompson, M. (2009). *It's a boy!: Your son's development from birth to age 18*. Ballantine Books.

Thompson, M., & Cohen, L. (2008). *Mom, they're teasing me: Helping your child solve social problems*. Ballantine Books.

Zucker, B. (2016). *Anxiety-free kids: An interactive guide for parents and children*. Routledge.

VIDEOS AND PODCASTS

Brown, B. (2010, June). *The power of vulnerability* [video]. TED Conferences. https://ted.com/talks/brene_brown_the_power_of_vulnerability?language=en

Damour, L. (2019, May). Anxiety and teen girls (No. 80). [Audio podcast episode]. In *Speaking of Psychology*. American Psychological Association. https://apa.org/research/action/speaking-of-psychology/anxiety-teen-girls

Jiang, J. (2015, May). *What I learned from 100 days of rejection* [video]. TED Conferences. https:/ted.com/talks/jia_jiang_what_i_learned_from_100_days_of_rejection?language=en

Prinstein, M. (2019, August). Why popularity matters (No. 87). [Audio podcast episode]. In *Speaking of Psychology*. American Psychological Association. https://apa.org/research/action/speaking-of-psychology/popularity-matters

Turner, E. (Host). (2020, October). Parenting through a pandemic (No. 107) [Audio podcast episode]. In *Speaking of Psychology*.

American Psychological Association. https://apa.org/research/action/speaking-of-psychology/parenting-pandemic

Zuker, B. (2017, May). Children, loss, and stress (No. 47). [Audio podcast episode]. In *Speaking of Psychology*. American Psychological Association. https://apa.org/research/action/speaking-of-psychology/children-loss

ONLINE RESOURCES

The following websites provide information and videos that offer useful tips.

BROOKS GIBBS HOW TO STOP A BULLY

youtube.com/watch?v=7oKjW1OIjuw

This video shows Brooks Gibbs presenting to an audience of teens, showing them how to respond to a bully, and not give their power away.

THE BOUNCE BACK PROJECT: PROMOTING HEALTH THROUGH HAPPINESS.

feelinggoodmn.org/what-we-do/bounce-back-project-/

This initiative from CentraCare Health website offers information and ideas on the five pillars of resilience.

PACER CENTER'S TEENS AGAINST BULLYING

pacerteensagainstbullying.org

This organization was created by and for teens, and offers advice on how to handle bullying and advocate for yourself and others.

STOPBULLYING.GOV
A federal government website managed by the U.S. Department of Health and Human Services. Contains useful information relating to bullying in schools, federal laws and civil rights, and cyberbullying.

DIY AND JOURNALING RESOURCES

If you are looking for additional writing-prompts, journaling activities, or workbooks, here are several excellent resources:

Gratitude Daily. (2020). *The ultimate middle school gratitude journal: Thinking big and thriving in middle school with 100 Days of gratitude, daily journal prompts and inspirational quotes.* Creative Ideas Publishing.

Journal Buddies. (n.d.). *Journal prompts for teens (and tweens).* https://journalbuddies.com/journal-prompts-writing-ideas/journal-prompts-for-teens/

Pellegrino, M. W., & Sather, K. (2019). *Neon words: 10 brilliant ways to light up your writing.* Magination Press.

Schwarz, N. (2021, September 7). 15 tips to build self esteem and confidence in teens. *Big Life Journal.* http://biglifejournal.com/blogs/blog/build-self-esteem-confidence-teens

Taggart, N. R. (2018). *Calm the chaos journal: A daily practice for a more peaceful life.* Chronicle Books.

MOBILE APPS

Sometimes an app can really help; so many kids find it natural to use an app to process emotions or get into a relaxed state. Apps can help

cue you to take steps toward a goal, such as doing a daily gratitude practice. Take a look at the list below and try one out; you may also recommend one to the grown-ups in your life:

CALM
This favorite app offers relaxing scenes and sounds, guided imagery, meditations, relaxation for bedtime, and other options that bring calm into your life. There is a free version and a paid version of the app.

365 GRATITUDE JOURNAL
This app focuses on positive psychology, optimism, and promoting daily gratitude practices.

HAPPIFY
Learn and practice activities that can help you combat negativity, anxiety, and stress while fostering positive traits like gratitude and empathy.

HAPPY NOT PERFECT
This app offers mind workouts, daily affirmations, and meditations to help you build confidence, manage stress, and promote sleep.

INSIGHT TIMER
Thousands of different meditations, relaxing imagery and sounds, and guided practices, including ones specifically for anxiety and for bedtime, are offered on this free app.

STOP BREATHE THINK
This subscription-based app helps you create a daily meditation practice and has meditations, journaling, videos, and even yoga lessons.

Bibliography

CHAPTER 1

Caliendo, M., Cobb-Clark, D. A., & Uhlendorff, A. (2015). Locus of control and job search strategies. *Review of Economics & Statistics*, 97, (1):88–103. https://doi.org/10.1162/REST_a_00459

Cobb-Clark, D. A., Kassenboehmer, S., & Sinning, M. G. (2013). *Locus of Control and Savings*. University of Bonn (IZA Discussion Paper No. 7837). https://ftp.iza.org/dp7837.pdf

Gale, C. R., Batty, G. D., & Deary, I. J. (2008). Locus of control at age 10 years and health outcomes and behaviors at age 30 years: The 1970 British Cohort Study. *Psychosomatic Medicine*, 70(4), 397–403. https://doi.org/10.1097/PSY.0b013e31816a719e

CHAPTER 2

Feltz, D. L. (2007). Self-confidence and sports performance. In D. Smith & M. Bar-Eli (Eds.), *Essential readings in sport and exercise psychology* (pp. 278–294). Human Kinetics.

Johnson, D. P. (1990). Indecisiveness: A dynamic, integrative approach. *Career Development Quarterly*, 39, 34-39. https://doi.org/10.1002/J.2161-0045.1990.TB00233.X

Kleitman, S., Stankov, L., Allwood, C. M., Young, S., & Mak, K. (2012). Metacognitive self-confidence in school-aged children. In M. Mok (Ed.), *Self-directed learning oriented assessment in the Asia-Pacific* (pp. 147-163). Springer.

Orth U., Robins R. W., & Widaman, K. F. (2012). Life-span development of self-esteem and its effects on important life outcomes. *Journal of Personality & Social Psychology*, 102,(6), 1271–1288. https://doi.org/10.1037/a0025558

Stankov, L., Morony, S., & Lee, Y. P. (2014). Confidence: The best non-cognitive predictor of academic achievement? *Educational*

Psychology, 34(1), 9–28. https://doi.org/10.1080/01443410.2013.814194

Vealey, R. S. (2009). Confidence in sport. In Brewer, B.W. (Ed.), *Handbook of sports medicine & science: Sport psychology*. Wiley-Blackwell.

CHAPTER 7

Pew Research Center. (2018, September 27). *A majority of teens have experienced some form of cyberbullying*. https://www.pewresearch.org/internet/2018/09/27/a-majority-of-teens-have-experienced-some-form-of-cyberbullying/

Royal Society for Public Health. (2019). *Social media and young people's mental health and wellbeing*. https://www.rsph.org.uk/static/uploaded/d125b27c-0b62-41c5-a2c0155a8887cd01.pdf

Weinstein, E. C., & Selman, R. L. (2014). Digital stress: Adolescents' personal accounts. *New Media & Society, 18*(3), 391–409. https://doi.org/10.1177%2F1461444814543989

CHAPTER 8

Delia, L. (2019). *Vibrate higher daily: Live your power*. HarperOne.

Helmstetter, S. (2017). *What to say when you talk to your self: Powerful new techniques to program your potential for success!* Gallery Books.

CHAPTER 9

Bluth, K., & Eisenlohr-Moul, T. A. (2017). Response to a mindful self-compassion intervention in teens: A within-person association of mindfulness, self-compassion, and emotional well-being outcomes. *Journal of Adolescence, 57,* 108–118. https://doi.org/10.1016/j.adolescence.2017.04.001

Bounce Back Project. (n.d.) *Resilience is made up of five pillars: Self awareness, mindfulness, self care, positive relationships & purpose.* https://bouncebackproject.org/resilience/

Dumont, M. & Provost, M.A. (1999). Resilience in adolescents: Protective role of social support, coping strategies, self-esteem, and social activities on experience of stress and depression. *Journal of Youth and Adolescence, 28,* 343–363. https://psycnet.apa.org/doi/10.1023/A:1021637011732

Shrivastava, A., & Desousa, A. (2016). Resilience: A psycho-biological construct for psychiatric disorders. *Indian Journal of Psychiatry, 58*(1), 38–43. https://doi.org/10.4103%2F0019-5545.174365

ABOUT THE AUTHOR

BONNIE ZUCKER, PsyD, is a licensed psychologist specializing in the treatment of anxiety disorders and related conditions. She is the director of Bonnie Zucker & Associates, a group private practice in Rockville, Maryland. She is the author of *Anxiety-Free Kids, Take Control of OCD, Parenting Kids with OCD, Something Very Sad Happened,* and *A Perfectionist's Guide to Not Being Perfect,* and the co-author of *Resilience Builder Program* and two relaxation CDs. She lives in Bethesda, Maryland. Visit bonniezucker.com.

ABOUT THE ILLUSTRATOR

DEANDRA HODGE is an illustrator and designer based in Washington, DC. She received her Bachelor of Arts in Fine Arts, concentrating in Graphic Design, from University of Montevallo. Visit @deandrahodge_ on Instagram.